Your Positive Baby Sleep Book

Your Positive Baby Sleep Book

Become confident with
your baby's sleep, feeding
& comfort from day one

Heidi Skudder

First published in Great Britain in 2024 by Yellow Kite
An imprint of Hodder & Stoughton Limited

An Hachette UK company

1

A CIP catalogue record for this title is available
from the British Library

Trade Paperback ISBN 978 1 399 72478 4
ebook ISBN 978 1 399 72479 1
Audiobook ISBN 978 1 399 72481 4

Typeset in Adobe Garamond Pro by Goldust Design
Printed and bound in Great Britain by Clays Ltd, Elcograf S.p.A.

The names and identifying details of some individuals
have been changed to protect their privacy.

Hodder & Stoughton policy is to use papers that are natural, renewable
and recyclable products and made from wood grown in sustainable forests.
The logging and manufacturing processes are expected to conform to
the environmental regulations of the country of origin.

Hodder & Stoughton Limited
Carmelite House
50 Victoria Embankment
London EC4Y 0DZ

www.yellowkitebooks.co.uk

To my very own gorgeous three children whom I love with all of my heart, and to all of the other babies that I have had the pleasure of having cuddles with. Your newborn journeys have taught me so much, and we now get to help thousands of other parents and babies too.

This book is for all of you. The sky is not the limit, it's just the beginning.

Contents

Introduction

I'd like to start this journey by introducing myself, given I will be the expert you have chosen to guide you through the beginning of your parenting journey. Parenting is like many other areas of life, in that there are multiple approaches and ways of doing things. What works for one family may not work for another, and vice versa. It can be overwhelming at times, particularly with the rise of parenting advice and experts on social media, and part of my reason for writing this book is to bring you lived- and experience-based ideas and solutions that will benefit both you and your baby in the so-called 'fourth trimester' (the first three months of your baby's life), and beyond that too.

My approach is simple: in passing my experience and knowledge on to you as a new parent, you can decide how best to do things – a way of parenting that feels true to you and your family set-up. There is no one-size-fits-all 'right' way to parent, but my approach to baby sleep is built from years of hands-on experience gained while working with thousands of babies. I have been a maternity nurse, breastfeeding counsellor and sleep coach for so many parents and families, in many different situations. Over the last two years I have also trained 47 others with my 'sleep school training programme', and these women are all now out in the world practising my methods and techniques, creating positive change for so very many parents.

This is a baby sleep book at its core, but really it is so much more. I love to use the term 'sleep-shaping', the idea of gently putting healthy sleep habits into place for your baby from the beginning, without any pressure or rules, and in a way that feels instinctively right for you. We will also explore some of the key pillars for your baby's long-term wellbeing. At first glance it may feel like a lot to take in but bear with me; the journey we will go on and the learnings you will receive about your baby will, for so many of you, be life-changing. If your baby does not fit the textbook mould of sleep, as is the case for so many, I will give you the confidence to fight for your baby and their comfort.

My desire is for this book to be a great big warm hug around you and your baby as you grow together and learn how one another works, guiding and supporting you on your way with expert knowledge and advice that seeks to enrich and improve your postnatal journey. Women are constantly disempowered with the (bad) advice of just having to survive the baby months, giving in to lack of sleep and losing themselves in the process – as if that is what motherhood is all about. The answer actually is no – motherhood can be so much more than assuming it will get better in time. You don't have to just survive those early months, you can thrive and your baby can thrive too.

My Story

My interest in babies was obvious from an early age. My mother was a childminder so growing up there were always small children around, and I played with dolls well into my teenage years. My genuine love for those dolls would go on to become a passion for the babies I looked after later.

At the age of 14, I babysat for my very first six-month-old baby for a whole day. I had no clue what I was doing, other than knowing that he needed to be fed and to sleep. Looking back, I think I still thought I was playing dolls, to be honest. I had my mum on the other end of the phone, and phoned her several times asking her what to do next. Like any new parent, I was learning the ropes and trying to work out 'my' baby. As the day went on, I began to feel more confident and soon I was working for multiple families in our village. Throughout college and then on to university, I spent every spare hour I had not on going out, but on babysitting and then, more formally, nannying. I think it is fair to say that being around babies came naturally to me.

I was able to turn that early experience into my life's aim to help families navigate with ease the sometimes rocky road that is the early years, offering my unique understanding of and expertise in the first few months of a baby's life – a time that is full of emotion, joy, confusion and, often, complete overwhelm.

I want you to love your experience of babyhood. They are not little for long and parenting IS hard, but it does not have to be so difficult that you lose all sight of everything from before baby arrived. There is so much that I want to share with you to help you on the journey.

How I Know What I Know

I moved to London in my early twenties and took on the role of night nanny while I studied psychology. I spent night after night looking after babies, which is when I realised that there was so much more to baby sleep then just being a 'good' or 'bad' sleeper. I spent hundreds of hours chatting to mums to keep them awake as they breastfed, sat on kitchen floors holding a breast pump to another mum's breasts while tears ran down her chest and she cried about how hard she was finding it. I sat and listened as new fathers talked to me about their lack of confidence with their baby and I prevented many a baby from going back into hospital because they had not fed for whole days or nights as tiny newborns because parents had not been given support or guidance. I have been part of countless different situations across many family homes, and each and every time I was honoured to be part of the journey. While those early weeks were hard for all of these parents, by the time I left a family when the baby was 12 weeks old, not only would the baby be sleeping well (often through the night), but also the parents would feel confident with both the baby's feeding and sleep routines, and in their role as new parents too.

As the years went by, I moved slowly away from the one and only baby routine that everyone knew (hello, Gina Ford), and started to use my own intuition and instinct with babies and their sleep habits. I developed a new way of easing into healthy sleep habits from the early days. I could see there were so many factors affecting these babies and I noticed patterns – from those who were more sensitive on dairy having worse cradle cap, or particularly sickly ones having shorter naps. There were patterns everywhere I looked, but no one was talking about them. Things considered 'normal' by so many – such as crying and broken sleep – generally all had a root cause. As I learned about formula milks and diets, and medications and specialist milks for reflux babies, I was able to go into families and not only get their babies sleeping, but make them happier and more comfortable too. Over time I built up knowledge that you simply cannot learn from a textbook, and I thrived in this role.

Why I Do What I Do

Armed with this experience, in 2011 I set up the company that is now Positively Parenthood (www.positivelyparenthood.com), my baby consulting business to help even more parents. I had spent most of my twenties staying overnight with parents and babies, and it was time for a change. I had always wanted to run my own business, so using my master's degree, I set up on my own. I have not looked back since.

'Nearly 13 years ago, we hired Heidi as a sleep consultant and we all fell in love with her. Our baby Mahlia had never slept well, and at five months old she was waking up every 15 minutes. We were broken, but I was scared of getting help from professionals as it made me feel like I was a failure as a mum.

From my first interaction with Heidi, I felt such a sense of relief and hope, and I knew we were in good hands. When Heidi first came to meet us, Mahlia was transfixed and I thought "she is a real-life baby whisperer!" Heidi transformed everything and we finally had a happy baby and could start enjoying being parents. I'm so glad she has now written a book!'

From my very first sleep consultation, I have loved every single moment. My client base grew, and I now consult on baby sleep and feeding with clients around the world, and run workshops all over London. Giving advice on how to have a happy, calm baby had become my one true love.

Even with the years of experience behind me, becoming a mother myself was not straightforward. After a difficult induction birth and antibiotic exposure, my first son developed reflux and multiple food intolerances. There was very little information I could find, so I tested different ways of doing things when it came to both his sleep and feeding. I worked with top paediatricians on his reflux, but ended up going in a different direction regarding treatment. I narrowed down the foods that triggered him and caused short naps, becoming my own reflux expert, with the situation repeated 18 months later with my second child. It seemed my children were sent not only to bring me joy and happiness, but also to further my understanding and knowledge of baby comfort levels and just how complex they can be.

Fast-forward to today, and my third baby has been much the same but with additional swallowing challenges, all linked to oral function. As far as babies go, she has been one of the most complex case studies even I have worked on. Yet, through all of this she has remained happy, smiley and a relaxed baby who sleeps really well (most of the time!).

While there is no one secret, the major overriding factor is a relaxed Mummy who has the knowledge – and knowledge is power – and the ability to make changes to their baby's wellbeing, including diet and feeding, in order to make them more comfortable. Three times over, my babies thrived because I was able to give myself sound advice and confidence about how best to deal with them. This is exactly what I do in my role as an infant sleep coach to thousands of other parents, alongside now training other women to do it too.

Why This Book Will Change Your Babyhood Journey

Being a parent today is hard. Parenting has always been hard, but add in financial pressures, a lack of childcare options, not living close to family support, and information overload from the good old World Wide Web, and many parents are hitting peak overwhelm. Every day, we are bombarded with information on social media and in the headlines that makes us question our every move as parents. Gut instinct and family support has been replaced with being told how to do things, left, right and centre.

In my role as a sleep coach, I am constantly hearing from parents who have a strong gut feeling that something is not quite right with their babies, yet they have been told that nothing is wrong, or their baby's behaviours have been normalised to the point where they then question themselves.

This book will change both you and your baby's experience of the fourth trimester. At the end of the first three months, you will have a baby who feels confident and secure in their sleep surroundings, allowing you as parents to maintain your work and social life, as well as your relationship, too. The fourth trimester is challenging and emotional. For those of you with easier, more contented babies, the sleep advice in this book will be invaluable for setting up easy and successful sleep habits and other healthy practices for life. If you have a more challenging baby, this is the only baby book that will actually make sense. Forget the generic baby routines and one-size-fits-all approach, this book will give you a true answer as to why your baby is not a 'textbook' baby. Not only that, but it will give you everything you need to know to make your baby a calmer, more contented baby, from strengthening your baby's gut and microbiome to establishing good sleep foundations.

The early chapters of this book are dedicated to your postnatal recovery and simply getting used to the idea of having a baby. There is zero pressure to think about sleep routines at the very beginning. When baby starts to become more wakeful, we start to look at simple sleep tips that can slowly begin to shape your baby's sleep. As your baby grows, week by week, we layer on additional options for introducing positive sleep habits without the need to leave your baby to cry. The middle chapters of this book focus heavily on ensuring that your baby is as comfortable as they need to be, in order to sleep well now, and in the months and years to come. In the final chapters, we explore key concepts in baby sleep, including making the most of your baby's nights, day naps and their ability to fall asleep on their own – something that is entirely possible for a healthy and comfortable baby, in the most gentle of ways.

Alongside my knowledge and experience, I encourage you to open up to your gut instinct. Pick and choose which parts of the book suit you and your baby best. Do not force something that you are not ready for. Explore your baby's wellbeing and be curious about topics that you may have been dismissive of up until now. In this book, rather than normalising babies who cry and do not sleep, you will end your journey with a baby who has solid sleep habits and the highest of comfort levels. This book is for you and your comfortable (sleeping) baby. Let's begin.

1

Preparing for Baby's Arrival

If you are reading this book before your baby arrives, then let me help you think about what you may need to do in preparation. No book or course can ever fully prepare you for becoming a parent, particularly in an emotional sense, but there are a few crucial practical and emotional considerations to think about ahead of your little person entering the world, and to get you in the best possible place for your baby's fourth trimester.

Safe Sleep Space and Co-Sleeping

There really is no need for fancy gadgets or expensive cots and cribs. All your baby needs is a safe space to sleep that meets the national guidelines of The Lullaby Trust, a charity responsible for educating parents on safe sleep to reduce the risk of Sudden Infant Death Syndrome (SIDS). Some of the most familiar options for baby to sleep in during the fourth trimester include:

✦ Moses basket

✦ Bedside crib

✦ Cot

✦ Bassinet

Fourth Trimester

The first three months after a baby is born is called the fourth trimester. This term was introduced by paediatrician Dr Harvey Karp in 2002, to help parents understand that although born to the outside world, their baby still relies heavily on their parents both physically and emotionally at the beginning. It is an encouraging term, used to help aid the connection of the mother and baby duo, including recreating a similar environment of comfort and closeness in this time, as well as to help new mothers understand the need to slow down and treat their new life with baby as delicately as the pregnancy trimesters themselves.

In the early weeks and months, your baby will sleep close to you, so having a basket or crib that you can move around your house can be really useful. This may be in addition to the sleep space you choose for night time next to your bed, or the same if portable.

You can also choose to let your baby sleep in bed with you, called 'co-sleeping'. The Lullaby Trust has specific guidelines for co-sleeping so do your research and decide which approach works best for you. It's worth saying that the reality is that, even if you choose not to co-sleep with your baby, when tiredness sets in or they become unwell you will likely share a bed with your little one. Therefore, learning how to do this safely is crucial. I surveyed 1,500 parents via my social media and found that 65 per cent had co-slept in the first three months of their babies' lives – either by choice or out of necessity. Co-sleeping is not for everyone but, when done safely, it can be a life-saver for many sleep-deprived parents, and, in some cultures is considered the only way to sleep with an infant.

Safe Co-Sleeping Guidelines

✧ Keep any adult bedding away from your baby, including pillows and duvets which can cause baby to overheat or be covered up.

✧ Place baby on their back to sleep.

✧ Do not have other children or pets in the same bed if you are co-sleeping.

✧ Ensure that your baby cannot get trapped between the wall and mattress, or fall out of the bed.

✧ Never leave your baby unattended in an adult bed.

✧ Do not co-sleep if you have been drinking alcohol, and consider your risk of co-sleeping when unwell.

Alongside your baby's sleep space, there really are very few basics that you need, though the below sleep aids and techniques can be useful from the very beginning:

❖ **White Noise** is used to recreate the noise that baby would have heard in utero with the whooshing of the blood to and from the placenta. Your baby has been used to hearing soothing background noise while they were inside your body, but after their arrival they are often being put down in a much quieter environment and still often expected to sleep. Not only is the environment quieter, but there are louder and sharper sounds (such as keys dropping) that would have sounded a lot more muffled when in utero. If baby is sleeping on you, they will still hear and feel your heartbeat, but if they are put down then they have no comforting noise to help them stay asleep. Using white noise on either a white noise machine or a device can be a helpful sleep aid for your new baby. White noise combines sounds across a number of frequencies, mixing them all together to help block out other sharper sounds that baby might otherwise hear.

❖ **Swaddling** is the process of wrapping your baby in a large muslin cloth or zipping them into a swaddle bag, in order to have their arms contained and closer to their body. This position of arms close to their bodies, or arms next to their head, replicates their position in utero. In the womb babies have little room to move as they get towards full term, and so are not used to having full movement of both their arms and legs. By swaddling baby, you help reduce sudden movements of their limbs that may otherwise wake them, and recreate the womb environment. Your baby can be swaddled from birth until they start to show signs of rolling, which is usually at 3–5 months of age. I prefer to remove the swaddle by around

12 weeks if possible, as swaddling for too long can cause baby to retain their reflexes which they need to grow out of for optimum physical development.

Building Your Baby's Gut

As we discuss later (see Chapter 10: Happy Tummy, Happy Baby), your baby's gut is one of the root causes of their temperament and contentedness in the early weeks, as well as influencing their sleep. A happy tummy equals a happy baby!

In the later weeks of your pregnancy, your colostrum will come in. This is the first breastmilk you produce, and contains dense nutrients, antibodies and stem cells that kick-start your baby's gut microbiome and immune system. To help you to build up a stash of this gut-boosting 'liquid gold' that you can give to baby post birth, you can start to harvest and collect your colostrum from 37 weeks gestation, although discuss this timing with your antenatal provider who will advise if your pregnancy and birth circumstances support this timing. By slowly massaging your breasts and attempting hand expressing, you will start to see a deep yellow liquid, thick in consistency, sit on the end of your nipple. Using small syringes, you can collect this and store it in the freezer ready for when baby arrives.

As well as boosting baby's gut, there is no harm in giving your own gut a little boost too in advance of giving birth. Your baby's gut is intrinsically linked to yours and by boosting your own you will be helping them out too. Most of us live busy lives and eating well in the late stages of pregnancy is not always possible, but probiotics, bone broth, kefir and other gut-boosting foods can ensure that your microbiome is strengthened ahead of its transfer to your baby when they are born.

What Is the Gut Microbiome and Why Does It Matter?

Your gut microbiome is a collection of bacteria, fungi and viruses that live in your body's digestive tract. Not only are these microbes responsible for how we absorb nutrients but they are also linked to our immune system and mental health. Having a healthy and diverse microbiome yourself can help contribute to your baby's gut microbiome, setting them up for the very best start in life.

Emotional Preparation

Perhaps the biggest shift in your world when baby arrives will be the emotional gear-change that happens when you become a new parent. It is an exciting time full of joy and anticipation, yet also overwhelming and, at times, it can be extremely challenging too. The expectations of what maternity leave will be like are, for some, far from what actually happens. Many parents will love having a break from work and immersing themselves in baby's world, but it is not uncommon to also have feelings of loneliness or having 'lost yourself' and your old life – and I say this with huge compassion and no judgement.

Having a baby means life will change significantly. The saying goes that 'nothing can prepare you for parenthood', but there are some factors to think about to help you in advance. Having an open and honest conversation with both yourself and together with your partner may help reduce the chance of mental health struggles after birth. Preparation is key in any area of parenting and no more so than for your mental health before and after childbirth. Helpful habits could include:

✧ Remembering to check in and communicate with your partner at regular intervals, no matter how chaotic sleep and feeding are in those early months. Sleep deprivation can have a significant impact on relationships, with one parent often picking up a greater share of night feeds and broken sleep than the other. Communicating your feelings to each other honestly and clearly can help stop resentment building up and encourages team work.

✧ If you are in a relationship where good communication can be patchy, try setting a weekly 'team meeting' – a time where you can open up to each other on how things are going and make any tweaks necessary to how the workload is divided up (including household chores, baby tasks and other life admin). Your main focus in the first months should be on your baby and some tasks will have to be set aside, while others will be delegated in a way that challenges your new dynamics. This is all part of your life changing to make way for your baby. Listing daily tasks and working out who will be responsible for which will help spread the load at a time where there are often high expectations on the person at home to 'do it all'.

✧ Keep expectations low while you navigate your journey into the world of parenthood. There are so many incredible benefits that come with being a parent. At the same time, your baby does take centre stage for a good while, so understanding that life will change and reducing the amount you expect to do, or get done, in a typical day is a brilliantly helpful way of feeling less frustrated. Some jobs will just need to wait. It matters more that your baby is fed and bonding with you than it does that the living room is dusted or the washing folded.

✧ There is simply less time for other areas of life once you become a parent. Rest assured that this slowly changes and you will have more time again. I often recommend that clients use the affirmation 'I am exactly where I am supposed to be', and recommend that they centre thoughts around the present moment rather than stressing about what needs to be done in the future. This is a powerful technique that alleviates stress and worry, and allows you to enjoy those precious first months with baby in the most mindful way.

✧ Have a discussion in advance with your partner about your ideas around parenting styles and approaches when it comes to sleep and feeding. Strategies to deal with your toddler or older child's behaviour can be addressed at a later date, but the two key areas of your baby's life to start with will be how they sleep and how they feed. If one parent is expecting baby to sleep in a bedside cot while the other is hoping to co-sleep, this could become a difficult conversation to have when emotions and hormones are fluctuating post birth. Are there any traditions that you are hoping to implement with your own baby? We often default into parenting in the exact same way as we were parented. For many of us, this is all we know. This may not be the way in which you really want to approach things though, or your childhood may differ significantly from that of your partner's. Communication and conversation are key components of effective parenting, both today and in the future.

✧ Understand that the idea of 'bouncing back' from having a baby is really not a thing. In fact, many postnatal professionals predict that women need anything from one year and upwards to recover from the birth of their baby. This includes both the physical and emotional recovery – your body will look and feel different and your priorities will change. Life will feel different.

'Matrescence' refers to the process of becoming a mother, and to the physical, psychological and emotional changes that a woman will go through. With every child that is born, a mother is born too, and this is a sensitive time, with ups and downs as you navigate the path of motherhood. Expect to feel different but do not be afraid to make plans to fit in life as you knew it too. The haze of birth and the first few weeks will pass at different times for everyone, and eventually you will start to see small parts of yourself re-emerge, but you will have grown significantly as a person too. It is only natural that you would look back to how life was, but bringing your focus to the now and having patience and showing kindness to yourself will be key.

Heidi's Journey

As I write this, I am in the throes of the fourth trimester myself. Although this is my third baby, with the juggle of two other children and working I struggled with the feelings of a loss of identity. This time around, I really felt as though I had lost the person I used to be and, on some days, would question whether she would ever come back. At times it would be hard to even brush my teeth, let alone have my 'normal' life back, and I felt really lost. This can be a lonely feeling, so do talk to those around you who are there for you – to listen and to hold your hand. Early motherhood is such an emotional time and it is entirely normal to have these feelings about your old life.

Alongside your emotional preparation and discussions, make sure to have lots of fun moments – and together with your partner too. Buy the cute babygro, design the nursery and send your partner cute pictures of things you'd like to buy for your baby or do with your baby. Bringing your own little mini you into the world, although challenging at times, is the most incredible experience. There is no love like the love you will have for your child, even with a fourth trimester full of sleepless nights and second-guessing your baby's cries. Know that you are not alone and that thousands of parents are going through exactly the same challenges. Reach out for support when you need it.

Summary

✧ You do not need expensive and fancy sleep gadgets to have a sleeping baby. Choose a safe sleep space for baby that is within your budget and works well for your family.

✧ Read up on safe sleeping guidelines; co-sleeping can be a game-changer for many families.

✧ Consider boosting your gut during pregnancy to help your baby's long-term gut health.

✧ Remember that becoming a parent requires much adjustment; communicate with your partner where possible and have discussions in advance around expectations and parenting styles.

2

The First
Few Days

Congratulations! Your baby is born and you are finally able to meet and get to know the little person you have been growing inside of you for the last 9+ months. While we hope that everyone gets the birth they have planned for, the reality is many of you will have very different births or experiences to that which you had expected. The emphasis, therefore, in the few days after birth is very simply on your recovery. Think about nothing else other than what YOU need, which will partly be dictated by the birth itself – everything else can wait. The only other variable you need to take care of is making sure that your baby is medically well and starting to feed – be that with breast or bottle.

If your birth has been straightforward, you may well have that rush of love and bond with your baby immediately. What is called a 'golden hour' after birth is the time in which your baby can be skin-to-skin in your arms or on your chest and possibly have a first feed. This time on the skin can also help regulate their body temperature and help with the transfer of your microbiome over to baby, helping build their gut and immunity almost immediately. This golden hour is recommended if your birth allows, but know that this special time does not stop at the first hour or day after birth. Skin-to-skin contact is a crucial part of baby bonding and feeding for weeks and months to come. Both yourself and your partner can do this at any time.

If the birth was more complex, with hurdles that you may not have expected, you may experience a range of emotions from shock to feelings of disappointment, or potentially not feeling anything towards your baby. Know that this is the experience for so many women. Lean on your immediate support network of midwives and your partner to help you and ask any questions that you need to in order to start to process your experience. Birth trauma is real, but time is a healer and slowly you will start to feel more for your baby. Seeking support from a professional or debriefing on your birth further down the line is recommended to help you process the event itself.

While you take your time to recover from the birth, be that in hospital or at home, you and your baby remain the immediate priority. Eat what you want to eat and spend this time however your maternal instinct tells you to spend it. Take your time to announce your baby's birth too. There is no rush – your baby will only be a few hours or days old once.

Think carefully about visitors and whether you feel up to it. Depending on your birth, you may not want anyone else to hold your baby in the early days and this is a normal protective maternal instinct which you need to prioritise. It is unlikely to matter too much whether a family member or friend meets your baby at two or five days old, but to you, as a very new mother, that difference in time may be significant in terms of your emotions. The change in hormones during the weeks after having a baby mean that emotionally you can feel fine one moment and very down the next. Not only that, but physically you may be in some discomfort which means that entertaining (even if a well-meaning friend) is not going to feel right for you.

Restricting visitors in the early days or even weeks of your baby's life can make a huge difference to your mental health and recovery, so do not be afraid to put yourself first. This is your experience and your baby – no one else's. You may find that your partner struggles more with this and may not understand your decision. This is quite common but does not mean that your needs are lesser. Whether you are excited and ready to show off your baby, or want to hibernate and not see anyone for the first fortnight, your feelings are totally valid. I urge you to roll with what feels right for you rather than buckling to any pressure from external family and friends who have not recently given birth.

If and when you decide to have visitors, remember that you get to choose when and what those visits look like. This is not about accommodating other people's timings and preferences. Push back on the length of visits or house guest requests that will bring more stress than support. You are the focus of this postnatal period. As a society today, we are notoriously bad at asking for help. Remember that anyone visiting a new parent who has not been a parent themselves (or is too old to remember) is unlikely to know that what you actually need is someone to unload the dishwasher or bring a meal to help you out. Although it may feel uncomfortable to do so, try asking for help rather than expecting others to know what you need. Any good friend or family member will be more than happy to help out.

Feeding in the First Few Days

Depending on where you give birth, and who is on duty at the time, the information you receive about feeding baby after birth

Useful Scripts for Saying 'No'

'We have decided not to have any visitors to the hospital when baby is first born, so that we can spend the first few days together as a family of three/four/five. We'll let you know when we are home and settled in.'

'We have decided to prioritise our baby's feeding and bonding in the first few days, so are limiting visitors until we feel on top of things. We will be in touch as soon as we feel things are going smoothly and you can pop over.'

'The birth was quite intense and I feel that I need some time to emotionally process what has happened with the help of [partner]. We are so excited for baby to meet you – please give us a little time to work through our feelings and we shall see you really soon!'

'We have decided to make sure that we catch up on sleep in the first few weeks while we can and [partner] is still at home. Once [partner] heads back to work then we can make a date and have you over to meet baby.'

'Thank you for thinking of us. Baby is doing well and we will make sure to get a date in the diary soon, once we have all settled into our own little routine as a family of three/four/five.'

'We would love to see you but life is quite hectic right now. We have decided the best time to come is between X and Y.'

may be very mixed. While some mothers will be recommended to wake their baby to feed them, others parents may not be given any specific advice on feeding and not be told to wake baby up at all. Advice will often vary from one professional to another and this will be a common theme that you find not only in the early days but throughout the whole of your parenting journey.

If you are bottle-feeding your baby, you can still use any colostrum expressed prior to birth in the early days to help boost your baby's gut. If you choose not to use colostrum or are unable to harvest any due to birth circumstances, formula-fed babies will need very small amounts of milk in the early days as their tummies are not able to hold big feeds. It is suggested that a newborn can hold anything from 5–30ml per feed in the first days, averaging around 60ml by one week of age. Bottle-fed babies are often satisfied after feeding with a full tummy, so you will likely find that you will need to wake your bottle-fed baby every 3–4 hours to feed them.

Colostrum is produced by your body in the run-up to birth and in the early days after birth too. Rich in antibodies and nutrients for your baby, it will gradually change to breastmilk by around day four or five. Until this point, the idea is that baby will survive just on colostrum itself. However, an often missed message is that for your milk to come in, your breasts need to be regularly stimulated. For this reason, I recommend waking your baby at least every three hours to feed in order to have them at the breast and stimulating your milk supply. When sucking at the breast, this sends a message to your brain that milk is needed. A baby who is sleepy and just left until they wake can become lethargic and not wake themselves, so it is important to encourage them to feed rather than assuming that they will ask for food naturally in the early days.

While most babies will be able to latch on to the breast and start their journey of feeding, some babies struggle to or are physically unable to latch, and this can be a problem if you are relying on your baby to stimulate your milk supply. In Chapter 9: The First

Few Days and Oral Disfunction, I will discuss oral issues such as tongue ties and lip ties, and also explain how babies can be born with 'muscle tension' which means that their head and body is compressed in utero, or in the birth canal during labour. This can have a direct impact on their ability to both open their mouth and also to latch. Unfortunately, body tension in babies is not something commonly discussed, so a baby is often labelled 'lazy' and some mothers may resort to bottles in desperation to get their baby to feed.

Should you find yourself in the position of having a baby who will just not go on to the breast, the first port of call would ideally be a lactation consultant who is qualified to assess for tongue tie in babies (your hospital should have lactation experts available to make an assessment about tongue tie and advise on difficulties in latching on). Do make your concerns known and ask for support and help at every stage – feeding is often difficult at first. Consulting a cranial osteopath may also be useful. In one session of cranial osteopathy, baby can go from not being able to latch at all, to opening their mouth and being able to feed more effectively due to the release of tension that has occurred during pregnancy or birth. It would be my dream that every baby receives a session of osteopathy after birth as this can have huge implications on their feeding journey, yet in the UK it is not something that many parents are aware of. Thinking outside of the box and acting early on your baby's latch can mean a more contented, sleepier baby and an easier journey for you both.

Supplementing Feeding in the Early Days

While you may be expecting a sleepy baby who goes to the breast and just does their thing, some babies are born wanting that little bit more nourishment before perhaps your body is able to produce it. If your baby is crying and seems very unsettled in the first few days after birth, first of all ensure that they are checked over medically and given the all-clear. Should baby still be unsettled and you are finding it difficult to catch up on any much needed sleep, particularly after a long birth or one where you have missed out on a night (or more) of sleep, you may want to consider a temporary solution to feeding until your milk comes in.

While colostrum is the cream of the crop when it comes to your baby's gut in the early days, sometimes a baby is simply not satisfied by that and will need a few extra calories until your milk comes in. In my vast experience of working with new mothers and babies, giving a bottle or syringe feeding in the early days to help settle a baby for a few hours can be the difference between a mother who ends up giving up breastfeeding early on because it is too all-consuming versus a mother who supplements for a few days or weeks until breastfeeding has settled down and then continues her breastfeeding journey.

Giving a bottle is often discouraged by many professionals but I have seen it become a life-saver for some mothers and should not affect breastmilk supply if done correctly. You should first offer baby the breast, so that your milk supply is stimulated. After the breast, you can then either syringe-feed or bottle-feed baby a small amount of formula or expressed milk (keeping the amounts small). In replacement of the supplemented milk, ideally you will also then hand express or pump so that your body understands to produce more milk (or to support your milk to come in sooner). Doing it this way means that your baby is used to the breast and your body is still stimulated to produce milk, but both yourself and baby can then sleep for a few hours afterwards before the cycle begins again. As your supply comes in, you can then reduce or stop the extra supplementing and move fully to breastfeeding if that is what you wish.

Heidi's Journey

When my first baby was born, I was in total shock. I had been induced, with a manual placenta removal in theatre where I was then separated from him for a couple of hours. I was emotionally and physically exhausted and I knew that, in order to get some rest, the best thing I could do was to be able to give my son a bottle. Recovery from birth is so important for your future breastfeeding journey, so I did what I needed in the short term, to make long-term feeding easier for me. With my second baby, I stored up colostrum and just gave my baby that until my milk came in, so he had no formula in the beginning. However, his birth was totally different – I had him at home and I felt full of energy afterwards. It just goes to show that each and every birth story can make you feel totally different and your feeding journey in those early days is likely to mirror that.

In my experience, nipple confusion of your baby preferring a bottle to a breast only really happens when baby is unable to breastfeed to their optimum ability, or is given too many bottles. This is exactly why ensuring that they are checked for tongue tie and any body tension is so important for establishing your breastfeeding journey. Babies with ties or tension can often show bottle preference from early on, as they find breastfeeding difficult.

Case Study: Baby Sophia, 3 days old

Baby Sophia was born via ventouse after a long and drawn-out labour, with Mum exhausted after four days of multiple induction methods and no sleep. Sophia was a big baby and appeared hungry, but would not latch on to the breast at all – likely due to being born with an induction birth, which causes stronger muscle contractions and therefore a possible build-up of body tension in baby.

On the postnatal ward, Sophia's mum kept being told to keep trying to feed, but was given very little help or advice as to why Sophia wouldn't latch, while being warned heavily against giving baby a bottle. While waiting to see an osteopath, and after three nights on the trot of Sophia screaming all night long, I supported Mum in giving Sophia a small amount of formula from a bottle. This gave Mum the first stretch of four hours sleep that she'd had in over a week. Both baby and Mum were more settled and, in the following days, Mum went on to continue trying to latch Sophia with the support of both a lactation consultant and osteopath. A few days later, Sophia was exclusively breastfeeding and there was no longer a need to give any formula. Mum later described how having a few stretches of sleep had helped give her the energy and confidence to push on with breastfeeding – a classic case of how giving a bottle or formula milk can actually save a mother's breastfeeding journey, rather than hinder it.

Summary

✧ Look after yourself first before taking into account anyone else's needs. This is *your* postnatal experience, and no one else's. It is fine to say no to visitors if you don't feel ready. Use my scripts to help you let people know your preferences.

✧ Reach out for breastfeeding support early on and know that much of the advice you receive will be generic or conflicting. Prioritise your rest and recovery, as this will get feeding started in the best possible way.

✧ A bottle given early on will not ruin your breastfeeding journey if done correctly. Sometimes it can be a life-saver for both your own mental health and your birth recovery. Be compassionate towards yourself in this time of uncertainty and focus on your baby's needs.

3

Can I Spoil My Baby?

While you are slowly recovering from birth and starting to look forward to your new life with your baby, it is normal to be met with feelings of doubt around how best to care for your newborn. We live in a world that tries to override maternal instinct by telling you how you should eat, take care of yourself and, of course, look after your baby. The rise of parenting accounts on social media has meant that information is now freely accessible to the new generations of parents. While this has been a support to so many, it can also prove to be overwhelming and, at times, confusing.

Baby sleep has always been an area of controversy, particularly among different generations who have all done things very differently. Parenting approaches have changed significantly to those used some 20 years ago. Today, with social media at play, opinions on baby sleep are being polarised to the extreme. This can be incredibly difficult when you are scrolling and seeing such a vast range of ideas and advice on your baby's sleep. Please don't forget that you have the choice to care for your baby exactly how it feels best for you.

One of the biggest questions that still sadly crosses many new mothers' minds as they start on their motherhood journey, is whether or not you can spoil baby. This question often stems from previous generations, who were told that they should put baby down to avoid them getting used to being cuddled and helped to sleep, approaches borne out of largely behaviourist approaches to sleep and childrearing. In one 1930s baby book, the advice reads 'never hug and kiss them, never let them sit in your lap'. The renowned US paediatrician Dr Spock then gave parents permission to hug their children in his 1940s parenting book, *The Common Sense Book of Baby and Child Care,* suggesting that parents use their common sense as to what their child may need.

Today, we know that there is no such thing as too much love. In short, you cannot spoil your baby and you should cuddle, kiss and hold your newborn baby as much as you could possibly want to. There is no harm in having your baby sleep on you, sleep next to you, or giving them all of your attention. Babies thrive on touch and connection with their parents. Let me reassure you that no matter what you are being told elsewhere, you cannot love or spoil your baby too much.

Contact Napping

You may have heard the term 'contact napping' – a popular way in which naps can be achieved in the early months and beyond. A contact nap is when baby is on you, 'in contact' as they sleep. This could be in a sling, lying on or next to you in bed, or simply just sitting and holding them wherever you are. These sort of naps will be very common in those early days and weeks while both yourself and baby adjust to the outside world, plus your baby will often just fall asleep wherever you are, with little concern for noise or what else is going on around them. Whether or not you then choose to continue with these contact naps past those initial weeks is dependent on both your own preferences and feelings towards contact napping and your lifestyle.

Contact naps have many well-researched benefits for both mother and baby, including:

✧ Lower cortisol levels in both parent and baby

✧ Deeper and more restorative sleep for baby

✧ Longer naps

✧ Bonding between parent and baby

✧ Rest and recovery for mother post birth

For these reasons alone, I recommend that you enjoy contact naps whenever you feel you can. Remember that holding your baby while they sleep is never going to become a 'bad habit' or affect the potential for them becoming a great little sleeper when they are older. Please never let anyone make you feel bad for wanting your baby to sleep on you. Some of your most precious memories will be of sniffing your newborn's head while they are in a peaceful slumber.

Though some parents are comfortable and happy to have their baby sleep on them for as many naps per day as needed, you may be one of those parents who finds it a little more demanding. The vast majority of us love a baby cuddle, but not everyone will enjoy having a baby on them for a large proportion of the day for months on end. This is totally ok. Most of my clients love the idea of having their baby sleep on them but just cannot do this all of the time, be that through the pressures of modern-day life, having other children, or through needing some space both physically and mentally. Becoming a new parent is all-consuming and life changes significantly; to then assume that you need to have your baby on you whenever they rest can be really overwhelming.

New parents today are more confused than ever about what they 'should' be doing with their baby and a recent big push in normal-ising contact napping has meant that a lot of parents are now feeling trapped in wanting to be able to put their baby down but feeling guilty for doing so. I mean it when I say that putting your baby down and having a minute for yourself is absolutely normal and they will still thrive and have a secure attachment to you if you put them into their cot or Moses basket for naps.

Not having contact naps all of the time may help when you need or want to:

✧ Spend time with other children

✧ Recover from the physicality of holding or carrying a baby for every nap (e.g. if struggling with a bad back/c-section recovery)

✧ Deal with other commitments such as work or needing to 'do' something during their nap times

✧ Feel touched out and need some space

✧ Want to catch up on house admin

✧ Take time for basic self-care such as eating a meal or taking a shower

There seems to be a shift in encouraging parents to forget the housework, know that this time won't last forever and stop trying to 'do it all'. The reality is though, that we are still having to do it all. As a society in the Western world, we are a long way off being gifted help from the government or any other source for our post-natal period recovery. Many new mothers are juggling a newborn, a home and often other children, and possibly a career too – even if not fully back into work mode. It is a lot, and our generation is expected to do more than any other when it comes to juggling. For this reason alone, give yourself permission to do what works best for you. If you want to hold your baby for every nap and that works, that is wonderful! If you want to grab a shower, have a few minutes of hands-free time or need to put your baby down to prepare dinner for your other child then that is just as valid. We need to move more towards understanding that every parent has differing needs and wants when it comes to bringing up their baby, and stop forcing one particular way of doing things on them.

Vern Hill, Carifit Founder & Babywearing Movement Expert

'One of the easiest and most comfortable ways to enjoy the freedom, convenience and developmental benefits of contact naps is to use a well-fitted baby carrier or sling. As humans we give birth to "carried young" and you may have noticed that your baby has their arms spread and knees tucked when they are on the floor, the exact position they adopt when held, carried or in a baby carrier. So here are three very quick and simple tips to help you both build confidence and comfort babywearing.

1. Get to know your carrier, its fit, clips, buckles or tie method and practise with it before your baby arrives. This will help you both to be more relaxed when using it with your baby in those early days.

2. Feed and change your baby before you pop them in the carrier, this will make you more comfortable and a satiated baby will settle and sleep far more quickly in the carrier.

3. Get moving as soon as your baby is in the carrier. Walk, sway or do Carifit (!) as it calms you both, reminds the baby of where they recently were and makes them feel safe. Ultimately it helps to foster fantastic early babywearing experiences.

Babywearing can remedy and rescue many situations so if all else feels like it is failing, feed them, pop them in your carrier and get moving to reframe the day.'

Dealing With Unsolicited Advice

It is one thing to decide that you want to hold your baby through their nap, or put your baby down for a sleep, whichever works for you, but another thing all together to have the confidence to answer other people's unwanted opinions on how you *should* be parenting. It is not unusual for family members or friends – and sometimes partners too – to comment on your way of parenting, especially when it comes to sleep.

Although well-meaning, you may hear comments such as 'you're spoiling her' or 'he'll never learn to sleep if you keep holding him'. Even with all of my experience in the baby sleep world, I have at times had to answer these comments from well-meaning family members. While you are very welcome to refer them back to this book, it may be helpful to have some possible answers up your sleeve for when this crops up.

Comments from others	What you could say in response
'She will never learn to sleep on her own if you hold her all of the time.'	'I am really comfortable giving her as much comfort as she needs while she is still so tiny.'
'We used to just put you down and leave you outside to cry a bit.'	'It is so interesting how parenting has changed over the years. We have chosen not to leave her to cry and want to be fully responsive to her needs.'
'You are spoiling her by holding her when she sleeps.'	'This is what works for us right now, but I appreciate that it isn't for everyone.'
'You were in your own room and napping by yourself from three days old.'	'Yes, I heard that babies used to be in their own rooms from early on. The advice now is for them to be with you until they are six months old.'
'You'll never get anything done if you keep carrying him around all day.'	'Right now, my priority is my baby. I am sure I will get back into doing things around the house when he is a bit bigger.'

Not only am I hoping that this book gives you everything you need when it comes to helping your baby to sleep well and feel comfortable, I also want to ensure that it acts as a big warm hug and gives you a dose of confidence so that you can parent in the way that feels instinctively right for you rather than being pressurised by social media posts or family members.

Remember, of course, that the early weeks are a rollercoaster of emotions and if you feel that addressing comments is going to worry you or make you feel wobbly, then an alternative could be just to smile and move on. Picking and choosing your battles and protecting your own mental health is key at this stage. You are ultimately the most important person right now, alongside your beautiful baby.

Summary

✧ There is no such thing as spoiling your newborn baby; hold, cuddle and respond to them in the way that works for you and your family.

✧ Contact naps have lots of researched benefits, but they don't just need to be on you – other close family members can also wear, hold or carry them to give you a break.

✧ Ignore any advice that doesn't sit or feel right for you and your baby. There will be so many opinions both online and from friends and family, but only you best know how to care for your baby. You are your baby's expert.

4

Recovering
From Birth

The early days, when you come home from hospital with your baby and embark on your new parenthood journey, is a time which should be protected. In today's fast-paced lives, it is easy to spend a few days at home and then rush to get back into things as normal, as life does not stop just because you have had a baby. Not only this, but we see images and videos of other new parents online, looking like they are out for fancy lunches or doing more than you are. This can leave us feeling down and like we are not enough, particularly at a time where our hormones are raging and crying may have become part of everyday life.

Remember though: this time is precious. You will not get back these first few special days and weeks together, and this is one of the rare periods in your life that you have a reason to slow down. Watch the box set, eat the cake and stare at your baby as much as you want. Life can, and will, return to normal before you even know it, by which point you will be longing for the days where you could stay in your PJs all day with an excuse not to get showered or leave the house. That can sound mad if right now all you really want is to shower and feel normal again, but I promise you that if you lean into this time, your future self will thank you for it.

Depending on the type of birth you have had, you may either be back on your feet very quickly or need to take longer out, possibly staying in bed for a little while more than originally planned. Regardless of how you gave birth, I would highly recommend the idea of the first two weeks being all about your recovery. Even if you feel ready to get up and about, use this time to slow down and make sure that you really are getting stronger. The idea of one week in bed and one week on the sofa has become a popular choice, and I talk from experience when I say that this made a massive difference to my own recovery. Spend the first week in bed and let your partner bring food and anything you need to you. Sleep, watch a series, and concentrate on establishing feeding by getting in as much skin-to-skin time as possible.

For the second week, stay in your PJs but move to the sofa (if your birth allows). You can be more engaged in everyday life within your house, but you are still able to rest and not feel the need to get out and about. You may want to go to the table for meals whereas before you may have had them brought to you, but otherwise keep things simple and straightforward. Baby cuddles, snacks and relaxing is your number one priority during this time. If you want to have visitors to see your baby this early on, then this is a great time to do so. Staying in bed for the first week also helps to stave off visitors too!

Recovery by Culture

While I try to convince you to take a mere two weeks out of normal life to slow down and recover from birth, in many cultures

Heidi's Journey

When I heard the idea of one week in bed and one on the sofa, I had already had my first baby and it felt almost over-indulgent in some respects. The more I thought about it though, the more my confidence grew in knowing it was what I needed and so I told my partner that second time around, this was the way we were going to do it. Not only that, but I suggested we had no visitors other than our parents and that they would only come once for a short time in the first two weeks. There was definitely pushback and not everyone was happy with my decision, but I felt protective of my family bubble and so made these decisions for me and my baby, rather than people pleasing for everyone else. It just so happens that those two weeks were everything I needed and more. It gave me the rest and energy I needed to then parent two children under two once my husband was back at work. I truly believe this period of rest and recovery should be prescribed to every new mother.

mothers are looked after far and beyond just the first two weeks of their baby's life. In Western countries, we often live far away from immediate family, meaning that it is harder to lean on them and get the support needed in those early months. We hear the phrase 'it takes a village' to bring up a child, yet once baby arrives and partners are back at work, usually after only two weeks of leave, we are left alone. Our fallbacks are often baby groups, local friends and, if we can afford them, paid professionals coming in to help, whether a cleaner, doula or food deliveries. Our village that once would have been our immediate family is now one that we have to seek out and, even then, it is not always easy.

Many other cultures have names for that initial postnatal period and the recovery process becomes somewhat of a ritual. In Latin America, *cuarentena* (quarantine) is the 40-day period post birth where the mother will rest, lay under hot blankets, take baths and refrain from any exercise, housework or sexual activity. A similar approach to postpartum recovery occurs in China where every new mother is expected to partake in the 'sitting month' – a period of keeping warm, resting and staying indoors, with relatives often delivering warm broths and meals to ease the load. The common theme among these cultures is that the mother's recovery is key, and there is no rush to return to normal life. Sadly, we are often much further removed from our immediate family now and so it is in your best interest to advocate and look after yourself. This starts with slowing down your pace of life and accepting that one week in bed and one week on the sofa is really the bare minimum needed for a speedier recovery.

Wishing Your Old Life Back

There is not one new parent out there that has not at some point (usually in the first three months) questioned why they decided to have a baby, or longs for their old life – or at least elements of it – back. While I appreciate that this sounds quite dramatic, the reality is that the fourth trimester is all-consuming, and you will likely lose yourself to a world of regular feeding, changing nappies, doing laundry and newborn baby chaos. This can be wonderful in its very own way, but also leaves little time to do even the basics that you were able to do before, such as eat regularly, shower and possibly even to leave the house.

When life changes dramatically, as it does with a new baby, there's going to be no magic answer to not losing your sense of self in the chaos. That said, having been at many new parents' sides as they have navigated this journey, as well as having done it three times myself, I know there is a lot that you can do to find yourself again. If you are prepared for this transition, then it comes as less of a surprise when you are sitting on your bed wondering if you will ever be able to dry your hair properly again. Knowing that you have options and guiding yourself through this change with kindness and compassion may include:

✧ When you are feeling particularly low and cannot see how life will ever change, know that time goes quickly. Before you know it, you will be getting out and about again, having a date night, or going for drinks with your friends. Life does come back, even if right now it feels almost impossible that you will be able to leave your baby and do these things.

✧ Try concentrating on what you do have in that moment, rather than those things that you are missing. It is ok to feel sad for your old life and, at the same time, be grateful for what you do have. In coaching, we would usually suggest writing a gratitude list of the things you are most grateful for in the moment. As a new parent, you likely won't even know where a pen is, so I would highly recommend just sitting, breathing and looking at your baby, using the mindfulness exercise later in this chapter to focus on the present. Your baby is amazing and won't stay little for long. There is power in learning to stay in the present, no matter how tough it feels.

✧ Take time to do something for yourself, even if that is only a 20-minute hot bath or hair wash. This seems insignificant to start with but small steps are a good place to start. That hot bath will soon turn into an hour popping to the shops, a dinner out and then, at some point, a day or night away from your baby (if you want or need this). These things can feel overwhelming but are necessary for your mental health and wellbeing in the long term.

✧ Encourage your partner to take some of the baby load, even if you want to do it all. One of the biggest sleep challenges I see with older babies is that they are unable to be put down to sleep by the other parent. This often stems from not building that partner's confidence at being involved with baby early on (possibly because they've not been allowed to). Especially if breastfeeding, you will quickly feel you want to be doing everything or that you are the only one who knows how to settle your baby. One of my biggest pieces of advice would be to let your partner try. Give them space, and time. Encourage them to have the baby for an hour here and there while you do something for you. This then makes leaving baby later on a much easier task.

It is common to feel resentment towards your partner when your life is the one that appears to have stopped and changed completely. Your partner, meanwhile, may be back at work after those first few weeks and still gets to eat lunch in silence (or eat lunch at all), chat to colleagues or friends during the day, and is able to listen to a podcast on the journey home – all things that you are not finding time to do. Communication is key. Make time to sit down together and explain your feelings. Expressed calmly, you will likely be able to come up with a plan for sharing the load a little more, which in turn will also help you feel more like 'you'.

Mindfulness With Baby – 10-Minute Exercise

Take 10 minutes out of your day to practise this mindfulness exercise with your baby. Find a quiet space, such as on your bed together or both lying somewhere comfortable on the floor, and choose some of your favourite relaxing music. This could be piano music or baby classical lullabies – whatever makes you and your baby feel most at ease. I recommend doing this exercise when baby is fed but not too tired, so that you get their best little selves. Mindfulness is all about being present in the moment, so take this time to put your phone away and focus solely on your baby. In the next 10 minutes, I want you to take in your baby, one body part at a time, starting with their tiny toes.

Looking at their toes, notice their tiny nails, the tiny creases in their feet and their little ankles. Feel their ankle bones and soft skin underneath their feet. As you take in these with your eyes, you can use your hands to gently stroke them too. Their little legs, then their tummy and back, their chest, neck, and chin rolls. Those little ears, their eyelashes and all the way up to their hair. With each part of their body, really focus and take it in, putting any other thoughts to the back of your mind and refocusing on your baby. While you do this, notice how your breathing slows and encourage long and deeper breaths, really filling up your lungs. This present time with your baby will be so special and much-needed time out from the high intensity of the first few challenging months.

Tips for Supportive Partners

As a partner watching from the sidelines, having a new baby can be a truly overwhelming time. Not only is your partner recovering from the birth itself, but it is likely that she is the main carer of the baby (especially if she has chosen to breastfeed). This can leave any new parent feeling like a spare part, wondering what your role is going to be in bringing up baby. When working as a night nanny, I had many a conversation with new fathers, often with mum out of earshot, and I can definitely say that it is not only mums that struggle emotionally at this time. Both parents are susceptible to mental health challenges and need support in those early months, with the non-feeding parent often overlooked.

As a non-feeding partner, even if you are not able to breastfeed, you can still take on a significant role in your baby's day-to-day life. Ways to do this might include:

✧ **Winding baby after a feed:** you may want to do some research on favoured winding positions (or read Chapter 6: Why Winding Is Essential) and even learn a mini baby massage routine. This gives you a little niche that is your own, and will also ultimately be incredibly helpful for your partner too.

✧ **Changing nappies:** it goes without saying that this can be a messy job but it's also one that does need to be done frequently. Changing nappies gives your partner some hands-free time to do something for herself too.

✧ **Settling baby off to sleep:** in those early weeks, it is likely that your baby will sleep anywhere, including on you. Helping settle baby to sleep and having a cuddly nap in the evenings is a lovely way of bonding with your newborn.

✧ **Taking baby for a walk:** this is perhaps one of the easiest options and brilliant for ensuring some one-to-one alone time with baby. Whether using the sling or pram, getting some fresh air gives you some head space and allows your partner some time to herself too.

✧ **Giving a bottle:** we explore this further in the chapter on feeding (Chapter 5: Establishing Feeding for Your Baby), but a huge advantage of introducing a bottle early is that you are also able to feed and bond with your baby.

✧ **Ensuring your partner is fed and comfortable:** while you may not feel it in the beginning, there is a huge importance in being the person to care for and feed your partner. Prepping easy-to-eat meals and ensuring lots of water is also at hand can be hugely comforting and takes one task away from your partner at a time where they should be resting and recovering.

You may find that your partner will not always willingly offer up baby. Perhaps she feels like she does not want to, or just does not think to. In this situation, you may need to advocate for yourself and know that this is important. Try verbalising how you are feeling and making a plan so that you both feel validated and able to bond with your baby.

Dads – according to the charity Tommy's, one in ten new fathers are now experiencing symptoms of paternal postpartum depression (with this figure likely higher as men are not encouraged to talk about their emotions). There are some brilliant resources now for new dads, and more men are speaking up about their experience of becoming a father. Make sure that you have someone to talk to when things seem overwhelming and you feel low. You could speak to your partner or a close friend or family member. Connecting with other dads who have been through the same experience as you can help reduce your anxiety. Knowing that others have felt the same is reassuring.

Having a baby is like no other life transition you will go through and your position as supportive partner can feel helpless at times. Remember to look after yourself. Although your partner's and baby's wellbeing is so important to you, you will have more patience and energy for support if you are coming from a place of self-compassion and care for yourself too.

Summary

✧ In the Western world, we do not prioritise a woman's birth recovery as many other cultures do. You have to be your own advocate, so keep life as calm and as simple as possible for at least the first few weeks, if not longer.

✧ It is really common to feel overwhelmed and to crave your old life back. Everything takes longer and seems harder with a baby in tow. Know that this is temporary and you will find your way again.

✧ Ensure that your partner is given the opportunity to help. If they are struggling, ask them to read this chapter for ideas on how best to help you. Communication is key, so keep talking.

✧ Accept help where you can; do not struggle alone and reach out for support as and when you need it.

5

Establishing Feeding for Your Baby

As well as a sleep coach I am also a trained breastfeeding counsellor and I can see how those roles can sometimes clash in the guidance given to new mothers. My hope is to relieve your confusion by giving you a realistic, rather than idealistic, picture of how sleep and feeding can intertwine.

My approach to feeding is as follows: if you are finding it easy to breastfeed and breastfeeding is going well, then brilliant, but if you are not enjoying breastfeeding, don't want to breastfeed, then use bottles and formula. There is zero judgement here on how you feed your baby.

How you feed your baby really is no one else's decision other than yours, so this is not a book dedicated to breastfeeding only. Nor will I be pushing bottle-feeding on you in order to help your baby sleep. Successful sleep is possible for both bottle- and breastfed babies alike, so the decision as to whether to breastfeed or bottle-feed needs to be made based on your family, your lifestyle and what you believe is best for your baby, rather than which feeding method you believe, or have heard, will make baby sleep best.

Breastfeeding rates are low in the Western world, and much of the reasoning for this comes down to the lack of support for breastfeeding mothers. Combine this with busy lifestyles and mental health pressures and it can be very difficult to start feeding your baby in alignment with your preferences. Breastfeeding is entirely possible for most mothers and babies who would like to feed, so with time and patience, as well as finding the right guidance and support, for which there are plenty of options available, you can have a very successful feeding journey. I am confident that this book will help play a role in both understanding your baby better, but also in supporting your breastfeeding journey too.

How Breastfeeding Works

Let's look first at breastfeeding and how you can get off to the best start with your milk supply. As this is not solely a breastfeeding book, I won't go into too much detail on the hows and whys, but there are a few major details that you need to understand to be able to feed your baby. In addition to this, there are many useful resources for you to draw on in the back section of this book, as well as your local community breastfeeding clinics and cafés, usually run by mothers who have breastfed themselves as a way of supporting and giving back to the community and other new mothers.

Firstly, breastfeeding works on a 'supply and drainage' basis. Simply put, the more milk your baby drains from your breast, the more milk your body will produce. This differs to 'supply and demand', as baby can demand milk from your breast but not always drain it properly. This is key information as milk is not just produced by your body without being 'asked'. Therefore, as I previously flagged in Chapter 2: The First Few Days, it is imperative that you put baby to the breast on a regular pattern of every 2–3 hours (more frequently if they are asking for it) to help stimulate your milk supply.

Not only do you need to put baby to breast, but you also need to ensure that your baby is able to latch on without causing pain, and drain your breast (transfer milk) efficiently during the feed. Babies who are unable to latch well, or at all, won't be able to drain (transfer milk) efficiently. As your supply is directly linked to breast drainage, this leads to your supply coming in slowly or being lower than you would hope for. This is why I would recommend that every new mother and baby duo gets advice on attachment and positioning early on. The smallest tweaks in the way in which you bring your baby to the breast can make a significant difference with your latch and milk transfer.

As well as the basics of attachment and positioning, it's useful to consider the baby's birth and position in utero, as well as their physiology. Babies born with tension carried from utero or the birth itself can be less likely to latch well, which may cause supply issues later down the line. By seeing an osteopath early on to release any birth tension, your breastfeeding journey is more likely to be successful. We explore this in more detail in Chapter 9, as well as giving advice on how to practise some exercises to help you along on your feeding journey.

In addition to body tension, tongue tie can also affect feeding, yet this is often missed in those early weeks, causing inefficient feeding and supply issues further down the line. Tongue tie is also discussed further in Chapter 9. For now, if you are at the beginning of your feeding journey and baby seems to be struggling with latching, a tongue tie assessment through your local antenatal clinic or seeking out a specialist would be a great starting point.

Breastfeeding in the Early Weeks

The majority of mothers will see their milk come in around days 2–4. This is when the colour of the milk turns from the thick gold coloured colostrum to white and thinner breastmilk. Depending on how your baby was delivered, this change could happen slightly sooner or later. Remember that the quickest way to help your milk come in is to stimulate the breasts by putting your baby to them. For this reason, if your baby will not latch at all, do seek help but also continue to stimulate your breasts either with a pump or by hand expressing.

If you choose to use an electric pump to do this, be mindful that there is such a thing as oversupply – where you can drain more than your baby needs and end up with too much milk. For this reason, be mindful to pump only as frequently as you are trying to put baby to breast, and for a short amount of time rather than leaving the pump on for hours. At the beginning, it is not about your output but rather about stimulating the breasts. Once your baby is latching again or more easily (usually after the release of tension and once they 'wake up' a bit), you will no longer need to do this as your baby can be doing it for you.

Assuming that you have a baby who will go to the breast and drink, I would recommend that you wake them and put them on to the breast every 3 hours in the first few weeks at least. Some babies are really sleepy to begin with and will sleep past this time if allowed. In the first few weeks, your main priority is getting your milk supply up and running. Offering the breast at regular intervals will positively impact your supply. Of course, if your baby is asking for a feed before this time, then you should feed them. Breastfeeding should be fully responsive, so if your baby asks for milk then give it to them – gone are the days where we have strict routines and regimented feed times for newborn babies.

Most newborn babies will need to feed every 2–3 hours, sometimes more at first, slowly stretching as they get older. There is no need to rush to feeding every 4 hours, which is often something clients ask about. Four-hourly feeding in the day time is largely linked to old-school baby routines which we no longer follow. You can easily implement a feeding routine as baby gets older (largely based around baby feeding every 2.5–3.5 hours).

If you are finding breastfeeding painful or difficult, or baby seems distressed, or you are feeding as frequently as every hour, then I recommend referring back to your local breastfeeding café or contacting a lactation consultant or midwife if still under their care to gain the necessary support to be able to help. There are also many online breastfeeding resources that can be a huge help, detailed in the resources section later on. Breastfeeding should be an enjoyable experience for both you and your baby, with no pain and discomfort associated with it. The reality is that it can sometimes take a while to get to that place.

Bottle-Feeding

Bottle-feeding is an important option for so many parents and there are a vast range of reasons as to why it is either a preferred or go-to option for many. Often, bottle-feeding mothers are overlooked as not needing the level of support that breastfeeding parents do. In reality though, a baby's latch on to a bottle should still be checked to ensure that they are able to feed optimally. Even when bottle-fed, a baby should be checked for tongue tie or any other latching concerns too. Issues such as body tension can affect a bottle-fed baby just as much as a breastfed baby, so seeing an osteopath can help baby feed to the best of their ability.

When starting out bottle-feeding, be mindful that your newborn baby's tummy is only small and they can drink too much milk, causing their digestive system to be overloaded. Depending on the formula you have chosen, always follow the guidelines for amounts on the back of the packaging. These guidelines are average amounts, so do not worry if your baby drinks a little under or over that amount. A baby who is fed and comfortable should wind and then settle down easily after a feed. If your baby seems to be unsettled both when feeding or sleeping then it could be that they are either drinking too much or too little, or perhaps the milk that you have chosen is not sitting right with them.

There are many branded formulas on the market and it can be a minefield to decide which you think is best for your baby. As a general rule of thumb, all formula brands have to be of the same quality to meet regulatory standards. However, within this, all formulas will differ slightly in terms of their added ingredients. Unfortunately there is no one formula that suits every single baby, so it is often a matter of trial and error. Start with a first milk (suitable for newborns) and then move on to another brand or type of formula should your baby seem particularly unsettled.

In order of preference, I tend to find the majority of babies are best on Hipp Organic Formula, followed by Kendamil, Aptamil, then SMA and Cow & Gate (this is nothing other than anecdotal evidence from my vast experience working with babies). When considering switching to a new formula, you can slowly switch baby over by changing the ratio of their current formula with the new one. For example, if your baby is on 150ml of formula (5 scoops of powder), you could initially do one scoop of their new milk, mixed with four scoops of their old milk. Transitioning slowly allows your baby's digestive system to get used to the new milk, and once on it fully you can then decide whether or not it is working for them. I recommend a minimum of five days on one formula before deciding to change again or switch back, unless of course there is a severe reaction in which case you should seek medical support.

Introducing A Bottle

We have explored how you use a bottle early on to help supplement feeding and support your breastfeeding journey. However, should your baby be reluctant and you find yourself in a position where you are not able to give a bottle, it can become incredibly stressful. Some mothers love being relied on fully for their baby's source of food, but others will need a short break, wishing or requiring to leave baby with a trusted family member or partner for a short period of time. Surely we are better off supporting mothers to know when and how to introduce a bottle, so that they have flexibility, instead of feeling stuck and then being forced into often stopping breastfeeding for that exact reason? Not being able to share the load of feeding can impact maternal mental wellbeing, yet as a society we are still lacking in any decent support with feeding in general, but even more so with introducing a bottle as it is still seen as 'interfering' with breastfeeding. Once again, my message is simple. If introduced well and in the right way, there is no reason why you shouldn't be able to do both – breastfeed and bottle feed.

The average age as a good starting point to introducing a bottle is often touted as around six weeks. I can understand where these guidelines come from but with clients I will often recommend introducing a bottle earlier than this. When you wait until six weeks of age, the reality is that a high proportion of babies refuse the bottle and then engage in an often lengthy battle with you, until one of you gives in.

Once your baby has reached two weeks of age, there is no reason you can't introduce one bottle a day to give you a break, or to help your partner bond with your baby too. It is hard for your partner to feel fully confident with baby if they are not able to be a source of food for them, and this has an added bonus of them being able to give your baby a bottle too. An evening bottle is often the preferred time of day for this as it allows partners to help when they arrive home from work, but if you would rather it is given in the day then do that (see Chapter 16: Combination Feeding for more information).

The most important points to remember when introducing a bottle for your baby are that:

✧ Breastfeeding works on a supply and drainage basis, so whenever you give your baby a bottle, you must also pump (express) in order to tell your body that you still need milk. If your plan is to switch to formula, then this does not apply as you can drop a breastfeed and replace it with formula. That said, supply is still establishing in the early weeks so my advice to start with would be to pump. This means that you won't drop any feeds in those precious early weeks that could potentially affect supply.

✧ The bottle's nipple works very differently from a breast, and bottles are generally much easier to drink from. If your baby has any difficulties with breastfeeding, including tension, a tongue or lip tie (see Chapter 9) or difficulty transferring milk from the breast, they may well prefer bottle-feeding. For this reason, you should work on breastfeeding challenges alongside introducing a bottle, or ideally before the introduction of a bottle.

✧ Babies who refuse the bottle are often babies with undiagnosed tongue tie or body tension. They are less receptive to taking the bottle and can become much more open to combination feeding once this is sorted (see Chapter 16: Combination Feeding for more information).

✧ The size and shape of the bottle you choose will often depend on your breast and nipple shape too. Ideally, the bottle you choose will be closest to your own shape and encourage baby to use their tongue and latch in an optimum way. By comparing the teat of a bottle against your nipple, both in terms of width, length and shape, you may be able to determine which bottle most mimics the shape and feel of your own nipple.

✧ Babies can transfer more milk, more quickly, from the bottle than breast, which can also contribute to a bottle preference. For this reason, you should stay with the smallest slow flow teat so that baby has to work harder for the milk. You can also choose to feed your baby more slowly by taking regular breaks and stopping to wind baby in between (known as 'paced feeding'), rather than letting baby take in the milk all in one go (see Chapter 16: Combination Feeding for more information).

Active Breastfeeding

One thing that often gets in the way of sleep for both babies and their parents is the idea that a breastfed baby should constantly breastfeed 24/7 and cannot be expected to sleep. Although the advice on breastfeeding varies from one professional to another, I find the general breastfeeding guidance of super-regular feeds and normalising cluster feeding (baby feeding frequently and around the clock, with very few or little breaks) as sometimes detrimental to not only the mother's breastfeeding relationship, but also on baby's sleep and comfort levels too (more on the tummy later!). For this reason, I like to recommend active feeding: meaning to keep baby actively sucking and swallowing during their feed rather than dozing and falling asleep. If left to fall asleep whenever they want to, the chances are that baby will often snack feed and then wake again after a short while having not taken a full feed. While this is totally workable for some parents, for others it can really get in the way of being able to put baby down at all. Active feeding helps a baby to take a fuller feed, therefore being more settled afterwards and hopefully sleeping better too.

The following feeding advice has helped hundreds of new mothers – this is an approach that I used often when I worked as a maternity nurse. I went into homes and helped new mums establish breastfeeding as well as healthy sleep habits for their babies, some of whom were only a few days old. I used this with my own three children and went on to breastfeed them exclusively for 4–6 months:

1. **Actively encourage your baby to feed while on the breast.** If they are not actively swallowing, then take them off, wind them, and put them back on again. One of the main causes of broken sleep for new babies and their parents is a baby who snack feeds and doesn't get full, then wants to feed again an hour later.

   A big part of active breastfeeding is to encourage your baby to stay awake and feed by using breast compressions to help stimulate the milk flow to their mouth. It is normal for baby to follow a 'suck, suck, swallow' motion and pause for a few seconds before then drinking again. But if baby slows down to the point where you feel they are suckling rather than sucking and swallowing, un-latch baby, wind them and then offer them to go back on to the same breast, or maybe offer the other breast if your baby was not swallowing much before you unlatched. This way, you are waking baby up a little to give them another chance to take on more milk. This helps baby take a bigger feed, stay fuller for longer and more likely go into a nice long sleep/nap so that you can both get some rest.

2. **Don't feel as though cluster feeding is your only option.** Very long and back-to-back feeds may be fine in the first few weeks while you have nothing to do and plan on resting and

recovering, but as life slowly starts to gets back to normal and you want to start setting up naps and longer night stretches, this can become a challenge.

For this reason, I would recommend feeding baby actively for up to an hour, but then after an hour giving baby a small top-up by using either the paced bottle-feeding technique (explained in more detail in Chapter 16) or syringe feeding if you prefer – giving baby small quantities of milk via a plastic syringe into their mouth slowly, until breastfeeding is more established). This allows them to be more settled on a fuller tummy so that you can put them down to sleep. Once baby is full and ready to go to sleep, you can pump for 10 minutes, to replace the top-up that you have given. As long as you replace any top-up with breast stimulation (by expressing or pumping) then there should be no issue with supply and feeding will eventually become easier. However, if you continue to give top-ups and do not pump instead, then you will find that top-ups will become something you have to rely on which could de-rail your breastfeeding journey. This plan may look something like:

✧ Breastfeed actively for an hour (or less), offering both breasts if swallowing slows down significantly on the first side.

✧ Offer baby a bottle top-up if still appearing hungry (if someone else can give to baby – great).

✧ Pump or express for 10 minutes.

✧ Baby is now full. You have also done your hard work so you can rest until the next cycle begins.

3. **Remember that the more bottles you give, the less likely baby is to want the breast.** While top-ups can be an effective

way of getting baby happy enough to sleep for a while in the short term, if you give them more than once or twice a day, you may then find that baby starts to prefer the bottle over the breast and this can cause breast refusal.

I find babies who have 1–2 bottles a day are usually fine when it comes to continuing breastfeeding well as long as their latch is not troublesome (e.g. issues with flow, latch, tongue tie and so on). If baby starts to have more than a few bottles a day and isn't getting on with breastfeeding as well, this is when there can be concerns about them going off the breast. For this reason, it is important to ensure that your breastfeeding latch is well-established from the get-go and consider getting outside support should you have concerns.

Top-ups or bottle feeds are so useful, especially to help you navigate the exhausting weeks post birth, but do pick and choose your timing. You are not trying to follow a definitive routine in the first few months, so choosing one sleep a day to focus on and put baby down for may be easier, using the top-up before this sleep if breastfeeding is not settling baby.

You could repeat this perhaps once again in the evening or the night. Prioritise using top-ups or bottles when they give you the most rest. You can deal with cluster feeding during the day far more easily than during the night when everyone is exhausted and needs some rest. Your milk supply is also lower in the evening, but gets better throughout the night so a bottle in the evening before you all go to bed would make the most sense.

4. Remember that skin-to-skin can be a powerful way of boosting your milk supply. If you start to feel you are having trouble with feeding and your baby having a full belly, then spend a night having them sleep with you and doing skin-to-skin contact. This often boosts your supply naturally. Also have a look at power pumping to help increase supply if you are not

happy to use top-ups, but want to try and move away from cluster feeding in the evening to get into a bedtime routine.

Above everything else, establishing your feeding relationship in those first six weeks will be key when it comes to sleep. If you focus on one thing, let it be feeding so that once you are ready to work on sleep, your baby is able to sleep well. A baby with a full tummy is a sleepy baby!

Heidi's Journey

None of my babies ever had hours of being awake during the night time, or long drawn-out witching hours in the evenings, and a big part of that was them being full and getting the milk that they needed from me, at each and every feed. I would focus on their feeding and never let them fall asleep halfway through a feed as I knew this would end up in snack feeding or cluster feeding (you'll find out later why this is not helpful for baby).

By using active feeding, they took as much as they needed, they were winded well and would then drift off to sleep afterwards and manage to go a good few hours between feeds. Learning how to position and attach a baby for breastfeeding is one thing, but understanding a feed in this way is equally as important in my eyes, for an easier and smoother breastfeeding journey.

Geraldine Miskin, Breastfeeding Expert

'When breastfeeding works, it is rewarding and so much easier than bottle-feeding. When it doesn't, bottle-feeding restores balance and brings joy back into your feeding and parenting experience. As Heidi said earlier, how you feed your little one is your personal and private decision to make, based on the challenges you experience and feedback your baby gives you. In order for breastfeeding to work, it needs to be comfortable, sustainable and effective for you and your unique family needs.

Many mums I meet feel like they have lost themselves in the process of doing 'what is best for the baby' instead of considering what is best for both of them. This in itself leads to breastfeeding becoming unsustainable and could end your breastfeeding experience sooner than you'd like. Consider what comfortable, sustainable and effective breastfeeding would look and feel like for you before your little one arrives. Then find the support, tools and resources to equip and enable you to create a feeding approach that works for you.

Getting ready before your baby arrives allows you to consider all your options before you are hijacked by exhaustion, hormones and emotions. You have options and choices to help you make the most of being a parent and enjoying your baby.'

Summary

✧ Establishing feeding is a crucial part of working on your baby's sleep. Feeding has to be going well for your baby to have the ability to sleep well.

✧ Body tension and oral ties can impact a baby's ability to both breast- and bottle-feed. Consult a recommended osteopath and/or lactation consultant who can help you get feeding off to the very best start.

✧ A baby who falls asleep on the breast isn't necessarily finished – encourage active feeding where possible to help baby take a full feed.

✧ Not all formulas are the same for each baby, so finding the one that works best for your baby will be crucial in helping them be as comfortable as possible.

✧ Bottles can be introduced early on in your breastfeeding journey if done correctly. This can help avoid bottle refusal later on.

6
Settling In: Weeks 2-6

If you have reached this chapter then you have successfully navigated the first two weeks of your baby's life and I want to send you a huge hug and congratulations. Giving birth in itself is life-changing as an experience, then learning how to look after a tiny baby is a major accomplishment, at a time when you are recovering physically and emotionally from the upheaval in all aspects of your life. There will have been tears of happiness, sadness and everything mixed in-between. Know that there is lots more of that to come, as you now begin to settle in to your new life together.

The end of the first two weeks can be a poignant time for new parents, in particular the mother. This is a time when, more often than not, the other parent is returning to work. In the UK, statutory paternity leave only covers up to two weeks for most men. This means that a new mother is often on her own at 14 days after giving birth – a very short period of time and by no means the full time needed to rest and recover. This can often leave mothers feeling wobbly and overwhelmed having had the load shared to a certain extent post birth. Going it alone (depending on your partner's working commitments) can be really daunting.

This can be a great time to seek extra outside support, having protected your baby bubble up until this point. Inviting a 'useful' family member to stay or investing in a doula for a couple of sessions a week can help you feel less in a panic when it comes to being on your own. These two options are not accessible to everyone, in which case try and make life easier by thinking about the following:

✧ Prepping meals in advance – having a new baby and everything that it entails means that even making your lunch can be unlikely to happen very often. You need ready-to-go food that only needs heating quickly, or even something cold that you can just grab and eat while pumping/feeding/rocking, etc. Cooking extra portions at dinner so that you have a healthy lunch the following day is a brilliant way of making it easy to get nutritious food. As is batch cooking, or buying in some easy to make/cook foods for the first few weeks.

✧ Ensure that you have very little to do other than care for your baby/other children. By this I also mean lowering expectations as to what else gets done on a daily basis. Whether it is the washing or the floors being hoovered – some of these things are just going to have to wait. Your priority is yourself and your baby, with other tasks within your world falling to the wayside until life becomes a little more manageable again.

✧ Make sure that you take moments to rest during the day time, or grab as many early nights as possible. While it is virtually impossible to follow the age-old advice 'sleep when the baby sleeps', actually you can find moments to rest, even if this is just lying next to your baby. I often found that by around six weeks of age, the post-birth hormones-high has subsided and this is when my clients started to complain of being more tired. Taking the odd nap or going to bed early can be really helpful to how you feel and function.

✧ Accept or ask for help where possible – this is something that is really hard for our generation to do. Asking a friend to come and hold the baby while you shower, or accepting the offer of bringing food over may seem like small gestures, but it is the little things that matter in this sensitive period.

While life ideally would remain slow and steady, for lots of parents things do have to slowly transition back to a more normal pace, especially if this is the second or third child with others to think about too. There is still no reason to panic over creating bad habits, or a creating a 'rod for your own back' with your newborn. As the first fortnight slowly turns into the first month and beyond, you should hold and cuddle your baby as much as you could possibly want to. At the same time though, you can also begin to 'practise' sleep training in the most gentle of ways, something I often refer to as 'sleep-shaping'. For some, this will start as early as week two. For others, the first two months will be a blur and then you will start to think about this. Either way, the emphasis here is on the words 'gentle', 'slow' and 'practise' – this is not about putting your baby down and leaving them.

From two weeks of age, or in the weeks that follow, I recommend the following to help gently shape sleep for your baby. These things may seem very basic but by putting the building blocks into place, the rest can follow as your baby grows. We keep expectations low in those earlier weeks, yet there are still things you can do to help your baby:

✧ First and foremost, focus on feeding. In these first weeks you will hopefully see a transition from lots of cluster feeding or struggling with feeds to beginning to go longer between feeds, maybe 2–3 hours if you are lucky. Use active feeding to help baby get long and full feeds, meaning they can go longer before their next feed. This will help when you start working on naps and a day time structure. Should feeding remain difficult for you in this time, then explore additional support from a lactation consultant or osteopath to find out what is bothering your baby.

✧ Waking your baby to feed at least every three hours during the day time (this means three hours from the start time of the last feed they did) if your baby is not waking for feeds and is still very sleepy in the day time. We want baby to know that day time is for feeding and night time is for sleeping, so waking them in the day will mean they take in more milk, and nights become longer over time as they are feeding well in the day time.

✧ Focus on this (rough) three-hourly pattern of feeding, awake time and sleeping. There is no need for exact timings when your baby is very little, e.g. starting your day at the same time or having set nap times. This puts too much pressure on everyone involved at a time when sleep and feeding can still be quite hit and miss during those early weeks. That said, a 'feed, awake and sleep' pattern happening roughly every three hours during the day can be a wonderful way of getting into the routine groove. There is no reason not to feed your baby to sleep if they then go down and sleep really well, but many babies will sleep even better if there is a gap between feeding and going to sleep, as they have had more time for the milk to settle and for any wind to come up. Winding is key for your baby and we explore this in more detail in Chapter 6.

✧ Start to put your baby down for naps every now and then after those first golden weeks of skin-to-skin and sleeping with you. This is not a hard and fast 'you must put your baby down and not spoil them' rule as we have already discussed. The low pressure practise element of putting baby down can, in itself, mean that they go on to become much more settled sleepers, rather than getting to an older age and never having been in their sleep space. This does not have to be for every sleep, but once or twice a day if you feel ready, make an attempt at popping them down in their cot or bassinet in the room that you are in (or try and have a nap next to them on the bed – you deserve rest too). Very often, they will just surprise you.

✧ Be mindful of awake windows (the time a baby can comfortably stay awake for before needing a nap/sleep) but don't be a slave to them. Awake windows are a really useful way of understanding when your baby is tired. Often, newborns are kept awake for hours on end with the assumption that they will then sleep better during the night time. The opposite is the case. Your new baby needs several naps, and often. The awake window for a baby in this 2–6 week period is around 60 minutes, sometimes just over an hour. If you can help baby settle to sleep at the end of this time, you will find settling much easier than if they have been awake for a number of hours. That said, please be very mindful that I do not want you to stress about these awake windows. Nothing bad will happen if your baby goes down later than their awake window. They simply act as a guideline for your baby.

Heidi's Journey

With my third baby, I was still in the throes of working out her tongue tie and feeding issues. This meant that my head was not in the game to worry or implement much of the sleep-shaping here that I otherwise would have done. Rather than stress and worry, I knew it was something I could come back to and just went with the flow. Your mental health matters as much as your baby's sleep, so make sure that you are choosing to do what works for the both of you.

The Five 'S's

When it comes to your newborn baby falling asleep in the early months, the key ingredients are their comfort levels and their calmness. Your baby needs to be free from tension and tummy ache as well as in a state of calm in order to fall asleep. Rather than any prescriptive methods to put your few-weeks-old baby down to sleep, we focus on them being relaxed. When a baby is in this state, sleep will simply happen.

The five 'S's were originally developed by Dr Harvey Karp in his *The Happiest Baby on the Block*, and are five supportive ways to help settle your baby, from crying to calm. These are brilliant tools to have in your back pocket in the early months of your parenting journey. All babies cry at times, so knowing how to deal with this in a confident and calm manner is essential.

When your baby appears unsettled, try just one or all of the following. They work in unison with each other, layering them together to create an effective way of helping your baby settle.

1. **Swaddling** – babies love to be swaddled and are not used to having their arms and legs flailing around, given the lack of space they will have had in utero. Using a swaddle bag or large muslin to swaddle your baby will often instantly calm them.

2. **Swaying** – a gentle bouncing movement from side to side is often an instant way of creating comfort. Remember your baby was used to a lot of movement in the womb while you went about your everyday life. For this reason, movement can be comforting for your baby. Some parents even find squatting to be a useful movement tool.

3. **Shh'ing** – your baby was used to the whooshing noise of the blood flow from your placenta in the womb. For this reason, they can be easily startled by sharp and louder noises in their new, often quieter environment. Using the sound 'shhh' or white noise for your baby can often help. Many new parents report that every time they use the hairdryer or stand near to the extractor fan their baby magically falls to sleep!

4. **Sucking** – naturally, most babies will have a desire to suck, which is often why they find the breast so comforting. If you are happy your baby has fed well but is still showing signs of wanting to suck, a dummy or your little finger are good options to help calm their nervous system. (Dummies should be used with caution, as they can produce a shallower latch for those babies who are yet to establish breastfeeding).

5. **Side** – while the current safe sleep guidelines (The Lullaby Trust) recommend babies sleep on their back to reduce the risk of

SIDS, when baby is awake they may often prefer to be held on their side. This often helps too with releasing wind, particularly if held on their left side. The 'tiger in the tree' hold is the most comforting to hold your baby in and can ease their crying when they are upset.

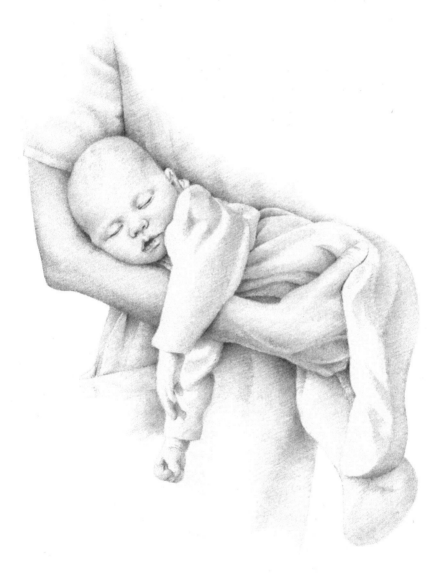

Case Study: Baby Theo, 5 Weeks

Theo's parents reached out when they were struggling with putting Theo down at all during the day time and finding that it was taking hours of him crying in the evenings to finally fall asleep. When we first spoke, we discussed managing expectations around his sleep given his age, but at the same time I knew that sleep could be easier for Theo and his family. We introduced a handful of gentle sleep concepts, including swaddling Theo as well as working towards age-appropriate awake windows (he was staying awake for hours on end, whereas he could only really handle an hour of being awake). Within days, his parents reported that he was a much more settled baby and could not believe how much sleep he was having. With just a few bits of advice, Theo's newborn experience was significantly changed for the better.

Night Feeding in Weeks 2–6

During the night from weeks 2–6, it may be the case that your baby struggles with going any longer than a couple of hours. It is worth concentrating on active feeding at night time too. I know how hard it is to stay awake and try and make sure that baby has a good feed, rather than dozing with one eye shut – I have been there three times over. If you can find it in yourself to ensure baby actively feeds, and do a nappy change in between breasts or halfway through a bottle, also ensuring that baby is well-winded and upright for some time afterwards, then you will see that baby starts to go for longer stretches rather than waking every few hours from having not taken a full feed or still having wind.

Until baby reaches birth weight, I would usually suggest waking a baby every four hours during the night during this time period. (If there are any concerns with your baby's weight then please follow medical advice given by your GP or midwife.) Once baby is up to birth weight, you can then start leaving them during the night. It is unlikely that they will go much longer than 4–6 hours (some will probably still be waking every couple of hours) but leaving your baby to sleep during the night (assuming no medical concerns) can help them understand that night is for sleeping, and that day time is all about play and being woken up to feed.

Summary

✧ Paternity leave in the UK is really short and when your partner goes back to work, this is often a time when having a baby can suddenly seem very overwhelming. Be kind to yourself.

✧ Try and accept help where possible and lower your expectations over what to expect. The house can wait, your baby is your priority.

✧ It is ok to need to put your baby down for a nap while you get on and shower or eat. Practising putting baby down can be a great way of getting them used to not always contact napping.

✧ Establishing feeding is still happening during the first six weeks. You may still be exploring your latch or making baby comfortable. Frequent feeds, including at night time, are very common during this stage.

✧ Learning how to settle baby using the five 'S's can feel empowering and help both you and baby become calmer. Sharing this information with your partner will also help spread the load when things are feeling difficult.

6

Why Winding Is Essential

We all take in small amounts of air when we talk or eat. However, some babies take in more air when they are eating or crying than they should. This is also called 'aerophagia' and it is the swallowing of air which leads to gastrointestinal symptoms. Not only that but babies who take in more air are also often more unsettled, they cry more and sleep less well too. All of these symptoms often lead to a diagnosis of colic or reflux (see Chapter 8) or, better yet, a baby who 'just doesn't like sleep' – all of which could be avoided with a reduction in air intake during their feeding.

The main issue with air is that if it goes in it has to come out! A baby's digestive system moves more slowly than ours as adults, so it can take time to go from one end to the other – leading to bloating, trapped wind and an overall feeling of being very uncomfortable. Not only that, but the air in a baby's stomach can try and escape back up, pushing the stomach contents on top of it back up with it. This often leads to posseting (baby bringing up small amounts of milk after feeds) or projectile vomiting in more extreme cases. Yet again, as a society we have normalised babies being sick, which means that no one really considers air intake as a reason for their baby's inability to be put down or sleep, or their overall happiness and wellbeing. We see it as part of a baby being a baby, when in fact posseting or vomiting on a regular basis is likely caused by some form of air intake.

Not only does the air in your baby need to come out – which often shows up as farting, hiccups, vomiting, posseting or belching – but it can also aggravate the digestive tract. When air sits in the digestive tract, it puts extra pressure on the digestive system, which can cause the gut to become angry and inflamed, having an impact on how well the gut then breaks down the food that is passing through. This is often why babies who take in air can also appear to be sensitive to certain food groups. They end up with an overall unhappier digestive system which has to deal with significant air intake being pushed through it.

Air intake as a cause of reflux is something that has only recently been researched and, therefore, until now has not been taken seriously by many baby and medical practitioners. In the last few years, there has been an increase in papers looking at aerophagia and its role in causing baby reflux and it now stands as one of the possible causes of not only a baby's reflux and colic symptoms but, in turn, their sleep issues too. Think about the last time that you felt bloated or had trapped wind and sleep became more of an issue; trapped wind really can stop you in your tracks. As an adult though, you are much more able to go and sit on the toilet, reach for a hot water bottle, take a supplement or go and lay on your tummy to help the wind out. Our babies simply cannot do any of these. Instead, they will often cry, where they then take in more air, and so the cycle perpetuates. When we then go to lie them down they struggle to settle and sleep, which is then normalised as typical newborn behaviour.

There are two parts to the issue of your baby and wind that

I would like to explore: the air intake itself and minimising air intake to help your baby become more comfortable and, secondly, helping your baby to release their wind. It is not always going to be completely possible to reduce air intake fully for your baby so you will need to act as your baby's best winding companion by ensuring that your baby releases as much as possible to be more comfortable and, of course, to sleep better – a scenario that you will both be much happier with.

Signs That Air Intake Is Causing Problems

Let's start with the air itself coming in to your baby. Air is ingested through the mouth, travelling down the oesophagus and into the stomach. This can be pushed back upwards alongside stomach contents, or be forced to make its way through your baby's digestive tract. This air comes in, primarily, alongside their milk. When they swallow milk, they can swallow air alongside it. Therefore, swallowing air has to do with how your baby is feeding – this includes both breast- and bottle-fed babies. It is a myth that bottle-fed babies don't swallow air or have latch issues, as this can exist with both.

During a feed, signs that your baby may be taking in air might include:

✦ Making a clicking sound on the bottle or breast

✦ Dribbling milk during feeding

✦ Choking, gagging or gulping at the breast/bottle

✦ Arching backwards away from feeds

✦ Refusing to feed or taking shorter than expected feeds

85

✧ Hearing your baby's stomach milk hit their stomach/a sloshing noise

✧ Sicking up

✧ Seeming distressed when feeding

✧ Sweating during feeding

✧ A shallow latch

These symptoms do not necessarily need to happen all of the time, and they can be incredibly subtle. As a parent, you may not even know that they are taking in air which is why it is often problematic to diagnose, with many parents unaware of any issues with their baby's latch at all. So how do we know it is air intake if the symptoms are mild or not at all obvious? The answer is often by looking at not just their feeding, but other areas that aerophagia may impact too.

Taking in air while feeding may have a knock-on effect on other areas of your baby's life. Most noticeably, the one thing that they do most of – or at least we would like them to – their sleep. If your baby's sleep appears to be broken, noisy or disrupted, and they are struggling to sleep for very long, then air intake could well be playing a part. A baby who is not fully comfortable and has trapped gas or wind may do very short naps, or not want to be put down at all, and ask to feed during the night time more than you would potentially expect them to. These all get passed off as normal newborn behaviour, but the reality is that a comfortable baby should be able to sleep well. We are born to sleep! So if our sleep appears broken and fragmented more than expected for their age, start with looking at whether or not you may be able to improve their latch.

Heidi's Journey

My baby daughter struggled massively with air intake during her early months and it became a real challenge for me as it had a direct impact on how easy she was to put down and also how long she slept for. I had this book to write and other children to care for and she would wake up after forty minutes from any nap and would let out multiple burps when I picked her up. It didn't seem to matter how much I winded her before putting her down either.

It started to become quite emotionally challenging as it seemed that no matter what I did, I couldn't help her. That was until we finally discovered and had her tongue and lip tie divided (see Chapter 9), and then things changed for the better. When they are so tiny, air intake plays such a huge role in their overall comfort levels, but it can be really challenging as a parent. Remember that things change quickly when they are so little and before you know it, you will be out of the eye of the storm.

Reducing Air Intake

Not only is air intake sometimes hard to diagnose in a small baby, but the getting help part can be even trickier. Very few health professionals and baby care providers are aware of the impact of air intake on a baby, particularly when it comes to their sleep. A latch is also often looked at from a very basic level. On so many occasions, my clients have been told 'the latch looks good', only to later be told that after further investigation their baby has a tongue tie or that body tension is causing a shallow latch. This is the reality of postnatal support – vast and confusing opinions, often from professionals who have not been educated in a baby's comfort levels or trained in looking for oral issues that can impact their wellbeing.

The first step should be to have a feeding assessment by a lactation consultant, ideally one who is fully trained in tongue-tie assessment. While sometimes it can be a matter of just a change in positioning and attachment during breastfeeding, often it is related to oral issues including tongue and lip tie. Therefore having someone who can help you assess breastfeeding, not only at a basic positioning level but deeper into the mouth, is essential. You can also contact an osteopath (or cranial sacral therapist) who can help you assess your baby for oral tension or also body tension that can be impacting their feeding. We explore this further in Chapter 9: Body Tension, Tongue Ties and Oral Dysfunction.

Making changes to your baby's feeding and the level of air that they take in during both breast- and bottle-feeding can be a long game. There is often no quick fix, which can become very difficult if you are struggling with feeding and sleep too. Finding the right person to help you can be challenging as aerophagia is still not fully recognised as an issue for babies. The answer is often not about a quick fix but a long-term commitment to oral exercises and slowly helping your baby relearn to feed in a different way with a deeper latch.

In the short term, here are some additional tips to help your baby to take in less air (useful for breast- and bottle-fed babies):

✧ When you latch your baby on to the breast, ensure that they get as deep a latch as possible. Pay attention to your baby's feeds, and try and stay present so that you notice their feeding and can take them off or reposition them if they fall off the nipple. When baby appears to have finished feeding, take them off and wind them.

✧ If your baby is bottle-feeding, make sure that the bottle works for them. Try a few different bottle brands until you find the one that sits best with baby. This will be both in terms of their latch, but also their wind after feeding and how much they then wind and posit.

✧ Formula-fed babies can often take in air just from the milk itself. When you mix formula powder with water and shake it, air bubbles appear and your baby drinks that down with the milk. Try stirring the powder into your baby's milk rather than shaking and see what happens.

✧ Always ensure that the very end of the bottle nipple is full of milk, so that your baby does not suck on air while they are feeding. Also take baby off the bottle before the last drop of milk so that they do not take in excess air at the end too.

✧ If using a prep machine for formula, make your formula by hand instead. This tends to reduce the air built up in the feed and therefore air intake.

✧ Keep baby on a slow flow teat for as long as possible. Although a faster flow will mean a quicker feed, your baby will usually take in less air if the flow is appropriate for their age and more similar to breast milk flow.

✧ Trial paced bottle-feeding to see if the slower flow helps your baby. Some babies will prefer not to be taken on and off the bottle as this increases their air intake, whereas others are better winded several times during a feed. Paced feeding is not a fail-safe yes for all babies, so it's worth bearing that in mind and using it to trial whether your baby is more comfortable afterwards.

✧ Try spacing your baby's feeds out. If your baby is feeding around the clock, they are probably not drinking effectively and therefore increased air intake will be likely. Try improving your baby's sleep between feeds, even if they need to be on you, and then feeding less frequently. This can be a game-changer for many babies and their comfort levels.

✧ A fast let down happens when a mother's milk flow is very fast and this can cause baby to guzzle in air and become uncomfortable. Pumping less frequently can help stabilise let down, but otherwise it is something that needs to be managed. Try using different breastfeeding positions including laid-back feeding positions as well as side lying. These positions enable baby to deal with a faster flow more efficiently. If a baby cannot handle their mother's milk flow, it is highly recommended that they are checked for oral function issues. Not being able to swallow and cope with feeding may be a sign that baby has a tongue tie or tension holding them back from feeding well.

Gut-Induced Wind

If baby is showing signs of being windy and possibly uncomfortable, then aerophagia is a great starting point to explore for your baby. However, it is not the only source of gas in your baby's body and it is as important to check in on whether or not the wind is coming from baby's gut too. When your baby ingests food that they are not yet able to break down, this can sit in the digestive tract and ferment – causing gas bubbles and wind. Another possible root cause of your baby's wind could be food groups or an unbalanced microbiome which we will explore in Chapter 10: Happy Tummy, Happy Baby.

Case Study: Baby Freddie, aged 4½ months

I first spoke to Freddie's parents when they had struggled to get any support from their doctors with his obvious discomfort. Freddie was regularly sicking up and struggling with sleep. Dad described Freddie as extremely windy and wanted help finding out why he was not a happy baby. During our initial call, it became apparent to me that Freddie was feeding very frequently for his age which could indicate one of a number of factors, but before making any big changes or asking his parents to spend money elsewhere we decided to focus on winding Freddie really well, in addition to spacing out his day time feeds. Freddie went from feeding every 1–2 hours, to feeding every 3–4 hours during the day time and his sickness dramatically reduced, plus his sleep improved significantly. Freddie was simply too full, and taking in so much air during his frequent snack feeds. He needed more time to digest his milk before feeding again.

Winding Techniques

While you work to sort out your baby's latch and possible air intake that way, we also need to look at how to help baby get the wind out. Not all babies burp easily, in fact, the most common myth within the baby world is that breastfed babies don't need to be winded. They very much do! And not just until they have burped once either. They need to be burped multiple times in order to bring up their wind, and this will vary from baby to baby. Some babies may just need a handful of burps to be released, while others might need up to twenty in any one given feeding period. Your baby's ability to wind themselves generally starts to develop at around 5–6 months of age, but even then you should ideally still attempt winding for them.

There are several classic winding positions that I find to be very helpful for bringing up wind, and other winding techniques that are perhaps less obvious.

Over the Shoulder Hold

This very common winding technique involves holding your baby over your shoulder and patting or rubbing their back. Patting can potentially break up any wind bubbles, so you are often better rubbing up and down to help release bubbles. Your baby's spine should be straight as the body will wind better this way. Any slumping may cause burps to stay stuck. This position also allows for slight pressure on the stomach to help.

Round and Round

This hold involves supporting your baby's neck by holding them underneath their chin and chest to ensure good head support. Again, your baby's spine needs to be straight so you can keep them upright with your other hand positioned on their back, rubbing up and down. rotate your wrists to move your baby in a circular motion. This helps to dislodge any stuck burps.

The Wiggle Hold

Hold your baby under the arms and up in front of you, with their legs dangling. This may sound like an odd winding position. In fact you are simply relaxing the body, in an upright and straight position, so that it gives any stuck wind a chance to come up. This is precisely why handing baby over to someone else is often when they end up burping!

Additional Winding Tips

There are lots of classic winding position holds to trial, plus many more organic ways to release your baby's wind. I would always recommend that you continue to wind your baby for as long as they are awake. This does not mean you have to sit and hold them specifically just for this but you can go about your normal day while incorporating some of these ideas:

✧ Walking up and down the stairs while holding your baby on your shoulder is often a fail-safe way of releasing extra burps.

✧ Tummy time is brilliant to put a little pressure on to the stomach and help wind come up. Try not to do this immediately after the feed, but once their milk has settled.

✧ Laying baby flat on their back for a few minutes and then picking them up again helps use gravity and is a great way of organically winding your baby.

✧ Holding your baby over your knee is another winding position that you will often find yourself putting your baby into.

✧ Simply sitting upright and letting baby's tummy settle can help with air bubbles coming together and then coming up when they are ready.

There is no one recommended amount of time that you should wind for – instead, just see winding your baby as a task that does not end. This is not said to stress you, but more so that you can see that winding has no end goal. No set amount of burps. Your baby will be the most comfortable for sleep if they have as little wind as possible. While we cannot fully control how much wind they take in or create, we can certainly understand the role that your baby's wind has in impacting them on a day-to-day basis.

Summary

✧ Babies taking in air while feeding is one of the biggest potential causes of them feeling uncomfortable and therefore struggling with both feeding and sleeping.

✧ Winding your baby during and after feeds, and then again in their awake time, is important. Don't just wait for one burp, there may be several more that come up.

✧ Winding positions can be useful to try, as can just laying baby flat and waiting for the wind to come out naturally as you go about your normal day time activities. Tummy time can be great for this!

✧ Ultimately, if baby appears very windy, then you will need to look into what is causing their wind; this can come from two sources, both air intake when they feed and also their gut producing wind when trying to break down certain foods.

8

Does My Baby Have Colic or Reflux?

Based on my experience working with clients over the last ten plus years, I know that the likelihood is that the majority of you will think you can skip this chapter. Perhaps your baby doesn't vomit and therefore why think about reflux? Or maybe your baby is mostly happy and therefore the idea of them having colic or reflux is just not in your mind.

Most parents know someone with an unhappy baby who endured a really tough time. By comparing your own experience, it's easy to think that your baby is fine as they're not as sick or as uncomfortable as a friend's baby. Over the years, I have worked with many parents who have dismissed their baby's symptoms, simply because they were not as bad as another baby's. Given that the majority of clients I work with have a baby who shows symptoms of reflux and colic, and one in four babies are said to struggle with reflux, I would urge you to read this chapter. I want your baby to be as comfortable as they can possibly be.

What Actually Is Colic?

Let's start with colic – possibly one of the most unhelpful words in the dictionary. Why? The word colic refers to a baby who is unhappy and cries a lot, with the NHS diagnosis being a baby who cries for three hours, for more than three days in a row. This is a lot of crying, and by this definition most parents will say their babies had colic at some point in the first few months. While colic does get better with time, it is not a rite of passage for every baby. A baby who cries is trying to communicate something to you. Your baby cannot talk and tell you that they have tummy ache, or need to poo, or are hungry, so instead they cry. By dismissing their cries as colic, we miss getting to the root cause of a baby's discomfort. Yes, you can wait it out until they grow out of it or you can address it head-on and have a more settled baby and, therefore, a more settled experience of becoming a new parent.

Unfortunately, we are still a society that deems crying babies, and those babies who do not sleep, to be 'normal'. When parents address these concerns with their GP, they are often (although not always) dismissed. In the worst cases, parents are told that they are worrying unnecessarily and asked 'is this your first baby?', making the suggestion that it is the parent that can't cope, rather than focusing on the baby being uncomfortable. I could talk for pages about parents I have encountered who have had to battle their way to getting support for their baby. While we are undeniably lucky with the healthcare system in the UK, the knowledge and under-standing of colic and reflux needs much work and this will take a huge amount of time to be put right. Parents continue to be told to either wait it out, or to manage or medicate the problem, rather than address the real reason as to why it could be happening. A huge part of my reasoning for writing this book is to reach more parents, giving you confidence to fight for your baby and their comfort levels, even if you feel dismissed.

Whether you have ended up with a 'diagnosis' of colic for your baby, or you've heard about it from another parent, I want to remind you that colic is not actually a diagnosis. It is a term to describe a crying baby. In reality, a baby with colic has something else that is going on and we can discover what that issue is. It may take some time and is always a process, often with no one magic cure. Nevertheless, we can help your baby on their way to a more settled day-to-day life, with easier and more settled sleep being one of our big end goals.

So what are the potential reasons for your crying baby? Using the process of elimination, we can work out what you need to do for your baby to become more comfortable.

✧ A vast amount of a baby crying is down to them being over-tired. Newborn babies have tiny awake windows and become tired and overstimulated very easily – all covered in Chapter 6. The very first port of call is checking in to see whether or not your baby might just be tired and, if so, working out how best to get them the sleep they need across the day time.

✧ Many babies get worse in the evenings as they have fed so frequently during the day time and their discomfort has built up. This is often related to them having wind. Aerophagia (see Chapter 7: Why Winding Is Essential) is super common as a cause of colic and hopefully by reading the previous chapter on wind and your baby, you will be well on your way to helping improve this issue.

✧ If you are breastfeeding your baby, there is always a chance that your supply is lower in the evenings. This is completely normal. Your baby will often then be unsettled and cluster feed to help encourage your supply to increase. Ensuring you are eating and drinking enough and using breast compressions (as discussed in Chapter 5) can help your baby get more milk. There is also the option of offering a bottle in the evenings, to rule out hunger being an issue – although don't forget that if you do, it's advisable to pump to ensure your supply knows to keep making milk. If you decide hunger is the case and your baby's crying and cluster feeding is no longer sustainable, then seek support from a lactation consultant who can advise on best practice to increase your supply.

✧ Babies who experience reflux symptoms (see page 101) tend to be more unsettled in the evenings. They often are not able to nap well during the day time, and frequent day time feeding can mean that their symptoms are worse by evening time. Reflux is one of the biggest causes of colic, and the causes of the reflux itself are detailed below to help you make sure your baby is more comfortable.

Spending time getting to the bottom of your baby's colic can be frustrating as every day there are multiple variables affecting your baby's sleep and feeding. However, through slow and steady elimination of the many variables affecting colic, my hope would be for your baby to become more comfortable, making sleep and feeding easier too.

Why Reflux Isn't Just About Being Sick

One of the main reasons many parents dismiss the idea of any reflux issue with their baby will be because the baby is not being sick. Most people believe baby reflux to be vomiting, or bringing up food or milk that is visible. While this is true for some babies, in my vast experience it is actually 'silent reflux' that is the biggest problem for the majority of newborns. Silent reflux is when a baby will regurgitate milk and stomach acid into their oesophagus but it stops short of their mouth, meaning you will not see anything come out of their mouth. This type of reflux can be one of the most disruptive to a baby's sleep and feeding but, without the obvious symptom appearing, is so often missed.

When looking at both visible and silent reflux, we need to look at not only one symptom of baby being sick, but a whole list of symptoms. There are over 40 symptoms to look out for in the table opposite. Looking at your baby holistically, in terms of their sleep and feeding plus overall wellbeing and health, we can build a bigger picture of what might be going on. It is important to note that these symptoms on their own can be signs of possible teething, illness, or for some of them, just normal baby behaviour (for example hiccups). However, when grouped together as multiple symptoms alongside broken sleep, feeding concerns and your instinct as a parent that something is not quite right, they can then be used to help come to a conclusion that baby could be struggling with some form of reflux.

Look at this table and highlight the symptoms that appear to be present in your baby's day-to-day life. Some of these on their own are nothing to worry about – for example, the odd bout of hiccups, or short naps if baby is happy. However, when baby is experiencing broken sleep or difficulty sleeping alongside a handful or more of these symptoms, we start to understand a possible level of reflux and then can go on to start troubleshooting. By addressing the root cause of the baby's reflux, we can make them more comfortable. After all, a comfortable baby is a happy and sleeping baby!

Windy baby	'Sicky' or posseting often	Projectile vomiting
Hiccups often	Congested	Coughing
Choking on milk flow	Gagging	Chewing lips/tongue
Smacking lips together	Refusing feeds	Pulling back on nipple
Taking a small feed then pulling off	Dribbling clear liquid	Acidic smell to mouth
Gulping during feeding	Hollow tummy churn sound	Sensitive gag reflex
Feeding little and often	Arching back	Appears 'super alert' (e.g. eyes wide and never sleepy)
Strong neck control	Straining noises	Noisy sleep
Dribbling milk during feeding	Unhappy on feeds	Sweating during feeds
Slow weight gain	Excessive weight gain	Dislike of car seat
Short or no pram naps	Dislikes pram	Banana shape to baby's body
Can't put baby down	Appears 'high maintenance'	Unexplained crying (colic)
Hard to get to sleep	Short naps	Waking when put down
Heavy reliance on sucking	Only sleeps well on you	Evening witching hours
Sleeping better at night than day	Very broken sleep (day/night)	Chewing on hands often

My Baby Is Showing Reflux Symptoms – Now What?

As much as it is important to point out these symptoms to help uncomfortable babies, we do not want to diagnose something that is not there. For this reason, I have created a framework I use with clients to get to the bottom of what is happening with baby and to assess whether or not we need to do anything. This framework is made up of three pillars that enable us to decide our next steps:

1. **How is baby feeding?** If feeding is going well and baby is putting on weight, then it might be that there is no concern and we can tick this box. But if there is any discomfort for baby or mother, or feeding doesn't feel easy, then there is probably room for improvement.

2. **How is baby sleeping?** Sleep is natural for babies. While a baby may need your love and comfort to get to sleep, they should still be able to stay asleep and be put down at times. When sleep feels difficult, broken, or it seems that something is stopping them from sleeping, then this needs to be looked at and can be one of the biggest, and sometimes the only, sign that there is something else going on.

3. **How is your mental health as a parent?** This is the one pillar that is so often missed in reflux support, but is crucial. How are your baby's feeding/sleeping and overall comfort levels affecting you? If your baby has mild reflux, but you are happy with them napping on you and they are otherwise mostly settled, you may not want to worry about any symptoms and just pass them off as normal newborn-ness, If, though, you are finding it hard to parent your baby as you can never put them down, or perhaps

their crying is making your days feel really tough, then you can 100 per cent do something about it. We have to think about ourselves too when it comes to our babies and being a parent. We simply will not enjoy the time with them if it is spent feeling miserable and down about the way in which it is going. There is always room for improvement, it just needs a little commitment of time, and trial and error from you. You can be both a happy parent, and have a baby who feeds and sleeps well – it's just that this comes more easily to some than others.

So often, reflux will show up most when we talk about sleep, as the body is unable to sleep well if there is discomfort going on. It is for this exact reason that I am confident in my ability to advise clients on baby reflux and will continue to do so until this information becomes more mainstream for both parents and medical professionals alike. By looking at sleep holistically, a sleep 'problem' that is often referred to as a behavioural problem, e.g. 'you have held them too much and that is why they won't sleep', is so often just a baby who physically cannot be on their back due to discomfort.

Heidi's Journey

I am a Mummy of three babies who all suffered from silent reflux and, although for all of them it was mild, it made a big difference to their sleep. Without the subtle signs that I was able to pick up on because of my experience, I probably wouldn't have known otherwise. They were all happy babies and they all enjoyed playing flat on their backs in the play gym. For each of my babies I took a different journey – medication, diet, tongue tie and air intake all featured in their early months. It does make those months of the fourth trimester more challenging and trickier to deal with, but you will come out the other side. Find other parents going through the same journey to share your thoughts and feelings with and remember that whilst it's difficult now, your baby will grow into a strong and healthy little human.

The word reflux can worry some parents but, as I explain to clients, it really just means some regurgitation is happening for baby and so we need to work out why. Once we have decided that baby is showing some of the symptoms of reflux and you are keen to move forwards with helping them become more comfortable, we can then start to look at the root cause. What is going on for baby that is causing these symptoms? Reflux has a cause, but the cause is not always easy to tackle and there are, more often than not, multiple causes.

Holistic Reflux Management Versus Medication

Looking at reflux as a symptom of something else going on is a newer approach in the baby world. When I cared for my first reflux baby, reflux was medicated and that was the only route available for most parents. Today though, approaching reflux with a more holistic view tends to be more popular and enables parents to understand their options before moving straight to medications.

Your baby should always be checked over by a GP or paediatrician should you have any concerns about their health, reflux or otherwise. The challenge lies in a baby who is potentially showing signs of reflux, but is otherwise putting on weight. A baby who is gaining weight well will often be dismissed by many doctors as not having any form of reflux, and their behaviour is normalised. Parents are told 'babies cry' or 'babies don't sleep' rather than listened to. Many doctors will not have a full understanding of the many possible symptoms of reflux that we have explored in this chapter, so will not recognise it to be the case unless they have specific experience of their own. Not only that, but the majority also still believe that reflux is caused by a weak valve between the stomach and the oesophagus causing the stomach acid to come back up, rather than as a side effect of air intake or food intolerances, as we know to be the case.

It is unusual for a doctor to look at the root cause of a baby's reflux and in fact the NICE guidelines for dealing with reflux actually suggest that a baby's symptoms should be managed, either by using milk thickener (see page 107) or medication, and only then, if symptoms still show up, should a dietary issue be explored. This means babies are sometimes being given medications such as PPIs (protein pump inhibitors), which reduce the stomach acid to make baby more comfortable, when they could be helped by other means before moving onto medication.

Medications certainly have a place for some babies, so they are not to be dismissed totally and, for many of my clients, they have been what was needed at the time to calm both baby and parents down before then attempting milk switches or any sort of oral tie procedures. Some of the situations in which medication may be needed could include:

✧ If a baby is refusing to feed and is not gaining weight

✧ If a baby is refluxing often and has a sore throat from the increased acid

✧ In situations where baby is screaming and inconsolable a lot of the time

✧ If one or both parents are struggling to manage with the lack of sleep

✧ If parents do not have the time or headspace to look into the root causes of reflux, for example with multiple children where change is needed quickly to help the wellbeing of the whole family

If your baby is projectile vomiting, is not gaining or is losing weight, is not feeding and appears unwell, or you are concerned about them in any way, seek medical help as soon as possible. In some instances, pyloric stenosis (a condition where the opening between the stomach and small intestine becomes narrowed causing severe vomiting often requiring an operation) can be confused with reflux and this requires immediate medical attention.

Using Milk Thickener

Another potential aid for reflux babies is to add a thickener into their milk if bottle-fed, so that they are less likely to experience the symptoms that cause issues, such as silent regurgitation and vomiting. These can be requested from your GP or purchased over the counter in many pharmacies. For breastfed babies, Gaviscon (designed to form a thickened layer on top of the stomach) can be given but if baby is not taking a bottle, this can be difficult to administer and often babies will spit it back out. While the idea of thickeners works in principle, it does not tackle the root cause of the problem. Many popular milk thickeners also have ingredients in them that can cause upset tummies and gut inflammation in babies. Therefore, while they may take away some of the symptoms of the reflux itself, they often cause other challenges in a baby's gut. These may be a useful stopgap for babies who are struggling to feed and not doing well with their weight, or if a baby is not swallowing well and struggling to cope with milk flow and you are working on their oral function challenges, but for those babies with mild to moderate symptoms a milk thickener is unlikely to be the answer. While you have the knowledge of the various options for helping your baby with their reflux symptoms, I recommend checking in with your GP or paediatrician to discuss your options.

Getting to the Root Cause

How quickly and easily your baby's reflux symptoms disappear will depend mainly on what the root cause is and also how much help you get with it.

The three most common causes of reflux symptoms are:

1. Aerophagia – the intake of air during feeding or crying, which then causes baby to be uncomfortable and forces stomach acid and milk up, when it needs to come out again

2. Body tension causing baby to be uncomfortable and 'squashed up', increasing their likelihood of reflux symptoms

3. The baby's immature gut, which can become inflamed, causing the rejection of certain foods and reflux-type symptoms

We use the term reflux almost as a label for what is going on with your baby as we dig deeper into what is causing baby's reflux symptoms, and then hope to reduce the majority of those symptoms. As it can take some time to pin down exactly what it is causing baby's reflux, this is where medication can sometimes play a short-term role.

In focusing on the specific symptoms relating to each of these causes in the detailed chapters within this book, my hope would be that quite quickly it will become obvious which path you need to go down. Many babies do have more than one of these issues and, as we will discuss in the next chapter, these can also be linked to each other. Take your time, keep patient and soon your baby will be on their way to becoming a comfortable baby.

Summary

✧ Colic is simply a word for a crying baby and will always have a root cause.

✧ A large proportion of babies who have colic have underlying reflux. Reflux is a symptom though, and there will be a root cause of the reflux too, usually either gut-related or connected to air intake.

✧ If your baby is experiencing any colic or reflux symptoms, you may find that their sleep is more broken or harder to achieve than other babies.

✧ Reflux can be managed both holistically as well as medically. There is no right or wrong way to deal with your baby's reflux symptoms and you should always take into account their feeding and sleep and, importantly, your mental health too.

✧ Reflux is usually a journey, with many factors to take into account, and it can take time to resolve and will feel frustrating at times. Look after yourself in the process as having a reflux baby is a very different postnatal experience to what you might have imagined.

9

Body Tension, Tongue Ties and Oral Dysfunction

As I write this chapter, I am acutely aware of this topic being one of the most dismissed when it comes to discussing and exploring a baby's comfort level. In the last few years, tongue ties and mouth breathing have become a widely talked about subject area in the adult arena. Popular wellness podcasts, books and experts are now focusing on how important these things are for optimum health and wellness. Yet many health professionals and baby care experts dismiss the idea that this is a problem for babies and small children. Before you do the same and skip on to the next chapters, I recommend you give this chapter a little of your time. Resolving any body tension and oral ties (tongue tie or lip tie) will make the biggest positive impact on your child's future. Tension and ties impact health and wellbeing in all areas, from behaviour to sleep and gut health to illness. It is vital to identify these issues as early as possible.

Body Tension

Tension is a word we associate with stress and putting our body under a lot of pressure. Babies spend most of their time snoozing on you, their little heads all floppy, with their delicate bodies relying on you for everything that they need. It may look and feel like your baby is not really under much stress, especially for those babies that are not crying much and who seem to be fairly chilled.

Mouth Breathing

When we sleep, our bodies naturally breathe through our noses. However, in some cases a baby will present with mouth breathing, which can be seen by an open mouth posture and hearing them breathe through their mouths. If baby has a cold or is temporarily blocked up nasally through illness, then this is nothing to be concerned about. However, when baby presents with consistent mouth breathing, this can be a sign of their upper airways being compromised. If the airways are narrowed, either because they are developing that way or because of allergies causing inflammation, then it makes it harder to breathe through the nose and baby must breathe through their mouth. Mouth breathing has potential knock-on effects to the child's longer term wellbeing but in the short term, can be a sign that there is body tension or oral function challenges, often but not always, related to tongue tie.

Nonetheless, muscle tension, the body's way of responding to stress – be that from birth or in utero – can exist in our babies when we otherwise would not expect it. When a baby experiences stress or difficulty then their muscles will respond accordingly, by becoming tightened and holding on to this tension.

To the naked parent eye, tension is not always obvious. If your baby is crying often and seems unsettled, then you may spot tension more easily in the way that they fling their head back and arch their body in discomfort, but you may well assume there is no tension if your baby is otherwise more settled and relaxed. Subtle signs of tension include:

✧ Clenched fists often

✧ Not wanting to lie flat

✧ Dislike of the car seat

✧ Furrowed eyebrows

✧ Baby appearing banana-shaped

✧ Head always turning to one side

✧ Dislike of tummy time

✧ Baby prefers feeding on one side

✧ Flat head

In many European countries, a baby will see a cranial osteopath as part of their postnatal care. In the UK, we are far off recommending this for babies, let alone it being included as part of the

NHS postnatal care package. Instead of helping parents get to the root cause of the body tension, we often normalise a baby's discomfort by telling parents that it is 'normal' for babies to not want to be put down. In the vast majority of cases, these babies actually are trying to tell us something.

If your baby is struggling with broken sleep, feeding and latching challenges such as air intake, if feeding seems difficult or baby seems unsettled in themselves, then an initial session with a cranial osteopath is highly recommended. If possible, find someone who works with babies regularly and really understands their anatomy (with some level of training in paediatric osteo treatment, as babies, and adults, bodies differ significantly).

Alexandra Freeman, Registered Osteopath

'The most straightforward birth can be a challenging event for both mother and baby. To journey from the uterus out into the world, a baby has to go through various movements to navigate the bony pelvis – they flex, extend and internally and externally rotate in order to arrive in the world. This tortuous descent can result in mechanical strains through the head and body, all while withstanding the pressure of the contracting uterus on the baby. Nature has brilliantly created a skull that is cartilaginous in nature – in a simplistic analogy, imagine a baby's head is a soft globe of cartilage within a membranous bag of jelly. Unlike adult skulls, the bones are not fused, and sit side by side. This allows the skull bones to overlap as a safety mechanism if the space in the birth canal gets too narrow. If the space has been restricted in utero or they get 'stuck' at any point along the journey this can result in an overlap of skull bones or an unusual shaped head.

Furthermore, if the expulsion from the birth canal has been difficult, and an instrumental delivery has facilitated the baby's arrival (ventouse, forceps), this can have an impact on how a baby latches and feeds, and even affect their ability to be settled. Within the cranium there are 12 cranial nerves with various functions – sucking, eye movement, nerve to the gut, facial movement – and these nerves exit between the skull bones to their destination. If there is any compression from any external force, be it a forceps extraction, or simply just getting a bit 'stuck' on the way down, this can have a knock-on effect on a multitude of functions such as feeding, lying on their back and being comfortable, digestion, and an ability to latch properly. For example, babies delivered by forceps will often have a marked preference for turning their heads one way due to the force exerted during delivery. This can make feeding difficult if they have to rotate their head the other way and they will have a breast preference. Caesarean babies will often struggle to adequately extend or drop their heads back as they have not extended their necks to travel under the pubic symphysis during a vaginal delivery. This lack of extension can impact the ability to open their mouths fully as they need to be able to drop their neck back in order to get a wide gape.

Often their heads will be flexed and this can impact latch-ing. Babies can also arrive a little 'squashed' if they may have shared space in utero with a twin, been engaged for a long time, or been breech.

Using subtle and often indirect techniques we can help restore the baby back to comfortable, address the strains that may affect their ability to feed well, and gently unfold them from their cramped position in utero.'

Releasing Tension at Home

There are some simple exercises you can try at home with your baby to help them ease tension and stress held in the body.

Tummy Time

Tummy time is the practice of placing your baby on their stomach, while they are awake and with you, to help them to stretch and develop key motor skills. By being on their stomach, the muscles in their body can stretch and release tension that may be there, which can then positively contribute towards baby feeding and sleeping more easily. Tummy time also stretches all of the muscles that may be tight due to tongue tie or tension, so is recommended before or after a tongue tie division, as well as being part of baby's everyday life.

Tummy time can also help baby develop motor skills, strengthen their neck and the ability to hold their head, as well as helping bring up burps and wind themselves, which is also useful before sleep time. The quality of tummy time is more important than the quantity, with babies ideally in an upright position over a rolled towel to help prop up their upper body and allow them to push up on their arms. A few minutes of tummy time in each awake window is a perfect amount of practice time and will positively support baby's overall development and learning.

The Guppy Stretch

The guppy stretch, also known as reverse tummy time, is another brilliant way to release any tension that your baby may be carrying, having a positive impact on their feeding and sleep, including their ability to use their tongue. As baby is gently placed into this position – either over a knee, towel or yoga ball – the space in their neck opens up, stretching their tongue at the same time. The guppy stretch can be used alongside tummy time at home to help release the muscles which can hold tension from in utero or birth itself.

Baby Massage

If your baby is calm and in a receptive state (not when they are upset or crying), fed and seemingly otherwise happy, you could enjoy short sessions of baby massage from home in order to help relax them and release any tension they are holding on to – just as an adult would benefit when they go for a massage. You do not need to be an expert in baby massage to be able to touch and lightly massage your baby, and there are many tutorial videos online if you would like a little more assistance.

Settle baby somewhere that is safe and comfortable for both of you and perhaps add in some relaxing music. Undress baby (you can do just their legs, just their arms, their chest, or their whole body) and speak to baby as you go through the motions. Choose a moisturiser or oil that is baby friendly, and hold out your hands in front of your baby's face as if to show them what is coming up next. If done regularly enough, they will start to get excited when they see your hands, knowing that what comes next is relaxing and bonding for both of you.

Baby massage is all about using soft and gentle strokes. Although there are specific baby massage routines for each body part, you can also just move your hands gently over your baby. The pressure should be light, but not too light so that it is tickly. Explore what works best for your baby, while also maintaining eye contact and calmly talking to them. Newborn babies will usually tolerate this for a couple of minutes, perhaps a little more. Don't forget that this can be stimulating for baby depending on their sensory need levels, so if they cry then stop. Finish with a nice feed and cuddle in the hope that they then sleep even better afterwards!

Tongue Ties

The journey of coming to understand tongue tie in babies has been somewhat of a significant one for myself, as a parent to three children. All three of my babies have had a tongue tie, so I am very familiar with the symptoms and how it can impact feeding and sleep. I am also aware of the difficulty in not only diagnosing but also in finding the right help and support for a tongue tie. There is a huge discrepancy in the understanding and treatment of tongue tie across the UK, which often leaves my clients confused and unsure about where to seek help. While I am not a tongue tie practitioner myself, I am often involved in that 'in between' process with clients, helping them work out where to go and supporting them with the knowledge around how a tongue tie could be impacting their baby, and in helping them seek out appropriate support.

One of the main challenges is that tongue ties are so often missed. The majority of health care practitioners that your baby will see in the first few weeks and months of their lives – including midwives, doctors, breastfeeding support workers and even paediatricians – will not have training in diagnosing a tongue tie. For this reason, many of my clients are very quick to tell me when we first speak that their baby does not have a tongue tie as they have already been checked. Unfortunately and frustratingly, it can often take several months of various opinions before a diagnosis. If your baby has been checked by a professional without the formal training, I would recommend you contact a tongue tie assessor (lactation consultants with additional training in tongue tie), a tongue tie practitioner, or a paediatric dentist. Even some of the very best practitioners in their fields do not believe in tongue tie, or believe that it doesn't cause an issue to a baby, assuming that feeding is going well and baby is gaining weight. However, as we are about to find out, tongue tie can have wider implications for babies as they grow older, other than just putting on weight.

The reality is that tongue ties have been around for as long as babies have been born and they are becoming more commonplace. In years gone by, a midwife would check a baby at birth for tongue tie and cut it there and then if necessary. It was part of a routine examination of the baby. However, with bottle-feeding becoming much more popular during the 1980s, this stopped becoming part of baby's aftercare post birth, leaving many parents to second-guess or seek external support if their baby had one, and the vast majority being missed. This is why now you will see online adults in their thirties talking about their own tongue ties and putting the pieces of the puzzle together. Tongue ties do not go away, they don't disappear and the body doesn't grow out of a tongue tie. They can cause long-term effects to an individual's health.

What is a Tongue Tie?

A tongue tie (also referred to as 'ankyloglossia') is a restriction of the band of tissue known as the frenulum that anchors the tongue to the floor of the mouth. If the frenulum extends forwards, or is too short or too thick, then a baby is considered tongue-tied. This can be assessed by looking at the movement of the tongue. When the

Heidi's Journey

I remember handing my baby over to the baby doctor on the postnatal ward after my first birth for his check and asking him to check for tongue tie. It had been something I wondered about, given he wouldn't latch at all to my breast in the early days. The doctor confidently said 'no tongue tie' and my heart sank. I needed a reason as to why he wasn't able to feed. A week later, after a lot of tears and emotional phone calls to breastfeeding experts that I knew, I self-referred to a private tongue tie practitioner and was told he had a 75 per cent tongue tie, which was cut there and then. Like so many of my clients, I assumed that the doctor or midwives would pick up on it. Thankfully we didn't lose too much of our postnatal journey to the issue, but I am aware of so many families that have only found out much later.

tongue is not functioning correctly, it can be concluded that baby has a tongue tie that then needs to be treated. Optimal tongue function contributes to so much of a baby's health on many levels, yet parents tend to be told that unless there are feeding concerns or trouble with baby gaining weight the tongue is fine and nothing needs to be done about it.

The tongue has a role in many of your baby's everyday bodily processes, not just limited to feeding. It was designed in such a way that it helps aid feeding, speaking and swallowing – there is an impact on so many of your baby's bodily functions. During a feed, if the tongue is functioning well, your baby is able to effectively transfer milk during feeds. The amount of milk your baby takes per feed is likely to be reduced if the tongue is not working as it should. This is not the only factor to take into account when looking at tongue tie but it is often the one symptom that will be taken seriously. If your baby is feeding well and putting on weight though, it certainly does not mean that they do not have a tongue tie – many babies will find a way to compensate for their tongue not working optimally and still be able to feed effectively.

As well as transferring enough milk, the tongue sitting in the right position will also ensure that your baby does not take in air while feeding. When working correctly, the tongue pushes the nipple of the bottle or breast to the roof of the mouth, meaning that your baby will suction properly, stopping air intake during feeds. By working to optimise the tongue, these symptoms are likely to be much reduced.

The tongue can also impact your baby's development too. When your baby is not feeding or cooing at you, their mouth would ideally be closed with their tongue resting on the roof of the mouth, against their palate. Babies with a tongue tie often have a narrow arched palate as the tongue has been held down and not been able to reach the top of their mouth, which helps widen the palate. Not only that but this position of the tongue also helps shape the jawline, as well as the airway structures, so a baby with tongue tie, and who mouth breathes, can develop narrow airways and this can cause not only increased mouth breathing, which has side effects of its own, but potentially more ENT issues and related illnesses too.

Finally, your baby's overall temperament and ability to relax and get into a restful state is also directly linked to their tongue function. The tongue should sit touching the palate, which in turn activates the vagus nerve, which is the longest nerve in the body and plays a role in the activation of not only the gut but also the heart and the lungs. When the vagus nerve is activated, we are in a state of 'rest or digest', which means that we are able to stay calm, sleep more easily and deeply, and also digest more effectively too (as opposed to the 'fight or flight' mode). This is often why babies who have tongue tie also struggle with digestion. Not only does the air taken in aggravate the gut, but the gut is also not able to function properly as the body is not in a 'rest or digest' state.

Symptoms of Tongue Tie

Many of the symptoms of tongue tie overlap with those that relate to reflux (as reflux can be caused by tongue tie itself, and when the tongue tie and remaining tension is dealt with, reflux symptoms often reduce too). If your baby is showing some of the symptoms below, I recommend a tongue tie assessment by a qualified professional.

Clicking	Dribbling	Pinching of the nipple
Falling on/off breast or bottle	Feeding aversion	Unable to create deep latch
Short feeds	Low milk transfer	Lip blisters
Crying at the bottle	Nipples that come out with a flat end after feeding (lip stick shape)	Long sleepy feeds

Never seemingly satisfied	Weight issues	Air intake
Slipping off the breast/bottle	Heart-shaped tongue	Cluster feeding
Open mouth posture	Bloated abdomen	Cracked/painful nipples

Case Study: Baby Otto, 5 Months

Otto first came to me with broken sleep and difficulty feeding at four months of age. After focusing on some basics, such as awake windows and a change in his formula milk, Otto was doing better but still waking up more than expected for a baby of his age. His parents were adamant on our initial call that his tongue tie had been checked by several midwives and they did not want to spend extra money on a third tongue tie consultation. After having covered all other bases, but with Otto still waking up frequently, I managed to persuade them to seek out a tongue tie practitioner in their local area. Otto was diagnosed with a posterior tongue tie and this was treated the same day. Within a few weeks of the tongue tie release alongside regular osteo appointments, Otto was sleeping not just better but through the night with fewer early wake-ups and longer naps. The difference the tongue tie made to his entire wellbeing was huge.

While one or two of these symptoms on their own may not be a concern, by looking at the whole picture of your baby's wellbeing, as well as considering your own gut feeling, you are able to build a bigger picture of what is going on for your baby. At this point, you can then assess what support you need to be able to help them move forwards and become more comfortable.

Tongue Tie Treatment

The quality of treatment for tongue tie in the UK differs vastly from one practitioner to another. When referring clients on to practitioners, it is not unusual to have to get a second or a third opinion, depending on the level of knowledge, training and research of each tongue tie professional. As one example, a recent referral for a tongue tie assessment saw a client coming back after being told that the baby has a tongue tie but that as it wasn't affecting feeding, nothing needed to be done. This does not take into account any of the future knock-on effects of having a tongue tie as a child or as an adult in later life, such as broken sleep, illness, narrow airways, allergies and much more too.

Many practitioners are also unaware of the link between reflux and tongue tie, given that the research into this is very new. For this reason, the baby may also be dismissed for treatment too. More commonly, I hear practitioners telling parents that there is no guarantee of any changes to symptoms. When faced with this decision, many parents then choose to not go for treatment as having their baby's tongue cut sounds painful. Cutting a tongue tie for a small baby is actually a fairly simple and pain-free procedure.

The best advice when it comes to finding the right person to help you is to find someone through a recommendation. You can also find details of practitioners from the Association of Tongue Tie Practitioners website (tongue-tie.org.uk). When booking an appointment, ask your practitioner about the impact of tongue tie – look for someone who recognises and understands the importance of the tongue function holistically, rather than just on the tongue itself. Moreover, as well as having a sound understanding of the tongue and its role within the body, you also need a practitioner who is going to provide both pre- and post-release exercises – these are exercises for both baby's body tension in general, but also specific movements of the tongue and massaging the wound itself in the mouth in order to help stop the tongue from healing back together again. The tongue tie appears and impacts development of baby from the first trimester in utero onwards, so once they are born your baby is already compensating for a tongue that doesn't function properly. They have learned to swallow and suck in a sub-optimal way and, therefore, will need teaching or retraining in those areas. This means that a baby will often need to undergo exercises and tension release before a tongue tie release and, crucially, after the release too. The very best practitioners will either give you follow-up exercises to do with baby or suggest that you work with an osteopath or myofascial therapist too. The tongue release is just a small part of the puzzle and, although symptoms may improve, it is the consistent and long-term release of tension alongside the tongue itself which will have the biggest impact on your baby's long-term health and wellbeing.

Tongue Tie Reattachment

It is not uncommon for a client to say they have already had their baby's tongue tie cut, but baby is still experiencing many of the symptoms. This is usually because the tongue has either only been partially released only, or has reattached itself. In my experience, I strongly advise working as a team with both your practitioner and an osteopath/myofascial therapist in order to have the very best results from your baby's tongue tie procedure.

Lucy Rayner, Paediatric Osteopath

'Once a full release of all fibres has been performed by an experienced professional familiar with paediatric oral function (paediatric dentist, paediatric oral surgeon, tongue tie practitioner), post-release wound care and rehabilitation with neuromuscular exercises are strongly indicated to strengthen the brain–tongue connection.

Suck training on a finger, elevating the tongue to its fullest height to encourage the tongue/palate contact and palate sweeps for palate shaping and reducing gag reflex sensitivity, and lateral tracking on the gum margin to promote lateralisation are among recommended intra-oral exercises to encourage the tongue to begin to move in all the directions it should be able to normally and reduce the risk of reattachment.

Low tongue posture caused by head and neck tension or mouth breathing from congestion may also lead to reattachment.

Encouraging the tongue to maintain its new full range of movement during the healing phase with lifting and mobility exercises should start directly after the procedure for best results due to the fast healing environment of the mouth.

A regrowth of the frenulum in the shortened position will restrict tongue mobility with scar tissue and potentially lead to a regression in symptoms or cause new symptoms to occur as a result of impaired tongue function.'

A Note on Lip Tie

Whereas tongue ties are being recognised as an important part of baby's journey more and more, a lip tie still remains somewhat of an unknown area. A lip tie, as with a tongue tie, is when baby's upper lip is held down against the gum by a thick or tight frenulum, reducing baby's ability to flange their lip outwards during feeding. If a baby has a lip tie, it is almost certain that they will have a tongue tie too. In America, a lip tie is assessed for alongside tongue tie, with a lip tie release often done at the same time. In the UK, however, we are not clear on the role of a lip tie in feeding, and with no research into this lip ties are rarely taken seriously. Anecdotally, I have had several clients who have had their babies treated for lip tie, as well as one of my own, and I have seen it improve feeding, for some significantly. The challenge with lip tie is that it is only released by laser treatment, of which there are fewer providers in the UK currently.

Do I Need to Assess My Baby for Tongue Tie?

With limited access to support services, and usually a financial cost to looking into tongue tie, it is unsurprising that many parents are reluctant to worry about their baby's tongue tie, or have an assessment done. As our healthcare system does not support the prevention of medical issues and rather just opts currently to treat any problems, it could be a long time before we see this as part of the mainstream healthcare system.

Heidi's Journey

My third baby's tongue tie was cut at eight weeks and while we saw a temporary improvement, after a week or so she seemed to go banana-shaped. After seeking a second opinion two weeks later, it was confirmed that the tongue tie had reattached and not been cut fully. We then had her tongue and lip tie lasered with an extensive aftercare programme, which finally made the biggest difference to her feeding and overall body tension.
I would love parents to know how important the aftercare and exercise is for every baby undergoing a similar procedure, as it really can make the biggest difference to their long-term health.

Dr Vatish Suraj, DDS, Paediatric Dentist specialised in TT

'The tongue is responsible for cleaning the oral cavity, swallowing, our speech, breathing, sleep and development of the teeth. We will begin to see compensations in all of these areas if the tongue's motion is limited by a restriction or a tie.

In infancy this will start from simple mouth breathing or sleeping when snoring. When the tongue is not touching the palate, the roof of the mouth, air is not allowed to be effectively inhaled through the nose. This will stimulate our sympathetic nervous system which is responsible for our fight or flight reponse and the release of hormones such as adrenaline and cortisol. These hormones are the root of arousal when it is not needed and manifest as hyperactivity, light sleeping and constant arousal. This results in our sleep being affected; when we are mouth breathing and snoring the amount of oxygen in the body is low, which leads to less time in REM or restorative sleep.

For children, this can result in bedwetting due to the body trying to achieve REM sleep by stimulating the parasympathetic system, leading to the the relaxation of urinary sphincter. Studies show that children with low amounts of REM sleep have a higher disposition to issues with focus, attention and performing simple tasks. In other words, imagine how you would be functioning on very limited sleep.

When I was a child, I was mouth breathing. I remember

when I was around five years old, I thought I should sleep with my mouth closed so flies wouldn't enter my mouth. By the time I was 12, I had a very crowded mouth with no room for my canines, I also had a very narrow palate. This meant I had to have four teeth removed to make space for my canines. I had never questioned it until I was 19 in my second year at dental school, I learned about sinusitis and realised I was suffering from it. This is also where I learned that the tongue is the best palatal expander and guide for the developing teeth. I then went to ENT where I discovered that I had a lot of allergies. Why is this important? Well, if I had had the correct assistance at the right time, I would not have needed extraction-based orthodontic treatment.

If the tongue sits at the bottom of the mouth due to a tongue tie or allergy, this can result in narrow palates, which affects breathing; we will then see higher incidences of crowding or malocclusion. If not treated early enough, this can affect your child's facial structure. Mouth breathing combined with a poor tongue position can mean your child has sleep issues, difficulty concentrating, crowded teeth and poor facial development, which can greatly impact your child's self-esteem. We would recommend identifying these issues early, to produce the best results. There are various treatment options: myofunctional orthodontics, tongue tie release and myofunctional therapy.'

Summary

✧ Tongue ties are widely misdiagnosed due to many health professionals either not believing in them or not being fully qualified to assess for them.

✧ If your baby is showing any potential signs of a tongue tie, it is recommended to have them seen by both an osteopath as well as a tongue tie practitioner.

✧ A tongue tie has the potential to impact both feeding and sleep, as well as the child's longer term wellbeing and development.

✧ Follow-up care and exercises are crucial when having a tongue tie procedure as this can stop reattachment and increase optimum tongue function.

10
Happy Tummy, Happy Baby

Your baby's gut holds the key to success in so many areas of their lives, as they grow from baby to toddler, school child, teen and then adult too. Their gut health can, in fact, predict their future. While it might not seem obvious right now, research is showing us, more and more, that the gut is directly linked to immunity, our physical health and, even more strikingly, our mental health too. As a society, we are only just scratching the surface about the role of the gut in our everyday lives, and therefore how to build a strong and healthy gut in those early days that aids and shapes your baby's future.

We know that a baby's gut is born immature and develops over the first few years of their lives. The first 1,000 days is a concept that is widely talked about in the infant gut health world, and this refers to the process of the gut growing and becoming more diverse in this time. When baby is in utero their environment is very stable and they are protected from the outside world. As soon as they are born they are suddenly exposed to all sorts of bacteria. This bacteria exists everywhere – from surfaces they touch to the air that they breathe. Each and every day the gut microbiome is changing and each and every baby's gut blueprint is different.

A baby's gut microbiome is fairly simple, containing many fewer types of microbiota (living microorganisms) than the average adult gut. Their gut is made up of different strains of microbes needed to break down milk in the early months. As exposure to milk, foods and environmental factors builds, so does their gut. New bacteria strains will be introduced and the gut then moves from an immature to a mature state after the first three or so years of life. This process is different for every single baby and experiences and exposure will determine to what level the gut builds, and how strong it is. When a baby has a strong gut and therefore a happy tummy, their overall temperament as well as sleep will look much calmer and easier. When babies have an unhappy tummy or are struggling with their guts, they are going to be more likely to cry more often, become unsettled more easily and sleep less well too.

Factors that can influence a baby's gut in the early days include:

✧ The mother's gut microbiota – this passes to the baby during at or around the time of birth

✧ Mode of delivery – babies born vaginally will receive a higher number of species of microbes to build their gut in comparison to c-section babies

✧ Exposure to breastmilk in the first few days – breastmilk passes a greater gut microbiome diversity on to baby

✧ Pre-term delivery – babies who are born earlier have been found to have a higher chance of gut dysbiosis (an imbalance in the gut)

❖ Exposure to antibiotics – although necessary for lots of important health reasons, babies exposed to antibiotics in labour or in their early weeks tend to be more likely to suffer with a sensitive gut

Some of these factors are simply not in our control. So often, birth happens differently to the way we both expect and want it to. The knock-on effect of this is intervention, stress and a delivery that is less optimal for a baby's gut. You might do as much as you can with your own gut in pregnancy, only to end up with a birth that was difficult and unplanned – antibiotics are used as a precaution in so many births. Your birth may have gone really well, but baby may develop jaundice and need to be given formula in order to help boost their body's metabolism and get rid of the bilirubin that causes the jaundice itself. Or, for your own mental health reasons, you may choose a specific type of birth or feeding method. There really is no judgement on any of these factors but where we have knowledge, we have power. Knowing that your baby was born via a certain type of birth or was fed a certain way in the early days can help inform us of where they are likely to be now with their gut and, therefore, what we can do to help them.

Boosting Baby's Gut

Your baby's gut is probably still in the super-early days of development, so there is much that can be done for them to help their gut develop and grow all of the good and useful bacteria they need in the microbiome. One of these ways is to introduce baby to a probiotic. Probiotics are live bacteria that are naturally occurring, which you can give in supplement form to help boost your baby's gut microbiota. There are many different strains of probiotics and differing products on the market so it can be hard to work out which one to use for your baby. Two of the most important strains to look for that have great gut-boosting properties for small babies include probiotics with *lactobacillus* and *biffido bacterium*. By giving your baby probiotics, you boost their gut microbiome and reduce any potential side effects of an inflamed gut such as wind, discomfort, food sensitivities, difficulty going to the toilet, colic and regurgitation. While probiotics are often not able to be recommended by many health professionals due to their research being new, they can be a brilliant aid for so many babies. In my experience, very few babies respond negatively, with most responding positively, with reduced symptoms that were otherwise bothering babies' sleep and feeding. Some of the more well-researched probiotic brands have excellent research behind them on probiotics reducing the number of hours a baby spends crying, regurgitation and reflux symptoms, and improved family quality of life.

Signs of an Unhappy Gut

More often than not, a baby's gut is not taken into account when they are suffering from colic and reflux-type symptoms. The idea that what a mother eats can be bothering their baby's tummy is seen as an old wives' tale by most people. Not only that, but we give our babies full dairy formulas without really taking into account the condition that their gut will be in, given their delivery and all of the other factors we have discussed that play a role in the development of their microbiome. A baby struggling with their tummy is often labelled as normal, with comments such as 'isn't that just how babies tummies are?' or 'it's normal for baby to be windy', and so on. We know that lots of babies struggle with their guts, but this does not mean that we have to just accept that.

If you have already determined that your baby is particularly windy, colicky, has symptoms of reflux, or just seems unsettled, then the gut is a good place to start. This may not mean it is the gut alone causing your baby to not sleep well but it is a huge part of the puzzle for so many babies and one that is so easily dismissed too.

Signs your baby is struggling with a sensitive gut include:

✧ Green or mucus poo

✧ Runny and foamy poo

✧ Explosive poo

✧ Constipation

✧ Crying when pooing

✧ Skin rash

✧ Cradle cap

✧ Baby acne

✧ Eczema

✧ Vomiting

✧ Posseting

✧ Reflux symptoms (see reflux list in Chapter 8: Does My Baby Have Colic or Reflux?)

✧ Unexplained crying

✧ Wind

Heidi's Journey

When I started out, reflux was just reflux and there was no link to the gut whatsoever. In fact, in those days if a baby had a dairy allergy, it was considered a completely separate thing from their reflux symptoms. As awareness has increased surrounding gut health, the two have become more interlinked, but many health professionals do not see it that way. After three reflux babies of my own, all with food sensitivities, I am glad to see more understanding of the gut and reflux being connected, but it can still often feel like a lonely place. Sometimes I feel people look at me like I am crazy when I talk about my baby and her reacting to foods and her tummy. I am met with comments like 'isn't she just having a bad day?', but when you know, you know. Gut health is something we should take seriously as it impacts our children's futures for the better.

Reflux and broken sleep are two of the biggest symptoms of a baby having some level of gut disturbance. Some of these babies will not show any skin symptoms or perhaps not have abnormal poos either. The problem with gut sensitivity and food intolerances is that they can so often be dismissed as normal baby behaviour. It is quite common for clients to be told that there is nothing wrong with their baby as they are gaining weight and do not have blood in their poo. While blood in the poo is definitely something to look out for with an allergy, the lack of it does not mean that the baby is able to happily digest everything. We have so much further to go when it comes to understanding the digestion of both breastmilk and formula milk for small babies, and there are only a few practitioners and baby care experts out there championing the cause – myself one of them.

Signs of an Allergy

If baby suffers from an allergy to a certain food rather than an intolerance or sensitivity, they are likely to show more obvious signs of there being a problem. A food allergy is triggered by a baby's immune system while an intolerance or food sensitivity is usually related to baby's digestion of a specific food. Allergy symptoms are (hopefully) more easily spotted and your baby should receive the adequate medical attention they need sooner, often including exclusion diets and changes in formula immediately. If your baby is showing signs of an allergy, then please seek help from your doctor, who will likely refer you on to a dietician or allergy specialist.

The table opposite lists the possible signs that baby has an allergy. They do not need to be showing all of these signs and on occasion they can be so subtle that they are missed. Babies can struggle with either an immediate allergy (IgE), which means that symptoms present themselves a few moments to an hour or two after exposure to an allergen, or they can be delayed (non IgE), which means that symptoms can appear anything from a few hours to 72 hours later. A delayed allergy can therefore be harder to diagnose, particularly when it comes to a rapidly changing diet of a breastfeeding mother.

Blood in poo	Vomiting	Rash/Hives
Crying	Broken sleep	Rubbing eyes
Dark circles under eyes	Coughing/wheezing	Congestion
Swelling of mouth/ throat	Eczema	Runny nose

The most common food allergy in babies is CMPA (cow's milk protein allergy) and this sort of allergy response to dairy in mothers' milk or formula can make for a very unhappy baby with many of these symptoms, but it can also be a delayed allergy response, which looks like a baby who is otherwise happy and well, but with a few signs that something is up, such as rubbing their eyes, broken sleep and dark circles under their eyes. Allergies should be taken seriously as they can be life-threatening, but delayed allergy symptoms are so often missed or passed off as nothing to worry about and all the while baby continues to be uncomfortable. If something does not feel right for your baby and you have been dismissed due to very subtle symptoms, seek further opinion from another source.

Intolerances and Sensitivities

Perhaps harder to recognise in your baby due to the symptoms often being normalised as newborn baby behaviour (spitting up, not sleeping and crying), intolerances and food sensitivities can be more of a guessing game. Whereas allergies will often present as obvious signs as per the table above, intolerances to food groups in babies are so often passed off as all part and parcel of baby having an immature gut. Rather than stopping foods in the breastfeeding mother's diet, or changing formulas, a lot of parents are told to wait it out – and that baby's gut will become stronger as they grow.

Whilst a baby's gut will get stronger over time, this does not mean that you have to just wait for their gut and not enjoy your baby in the meantime.

An intolerance or food sensitivity is not an immune system response like an allergy is, but it is to do with the digestive system not fully being able to handle the breakdown of that food as it stands. This does not mean that baby will never be able to digest and break down this food, but that currently for whatever reason (birth, antibiotics, gestational age and so on), they are not able to and this is causing them some discomfort. Their digestive system may not have the necessary enzymes needed to break down that food, or they may have a sensitivity to certain food groups, causing inflammation of the gut and therefore an unhappy digestive tract.

I want you to imagine for a moment that you were struggling to sleep on the nights that you ate pasta for dinner. You noticed your sleep was lighter, you tossed and turned a lot and your tummy felt bloated. As adults, we would recognise this as being linked, keep a food diary and then make the necessary change to become more comfortable. However, in babies, we just pass off bad nights as exactly that, bad nights. Our babies are able to tell us so much more about their body via their behaviour, including their temperament when they are awake, their sleep and their overall wellbeing.

Dealing With an Unhappy Gut – Your Next Steps

Once you have decided that your baby is struggling with their tummy, and you have ruled out air intake as being the cause of their discomfort, you can start to make changes that will help settle the gut to become more comfortable. Please do understand that this is not a quick fix for your baby and we often refer to getting to the root cause as a journey. If your baby's gut is unsettled, then they need time for this to heal. It can take a number of weeks or months for your baby's gut to fully recover from being inflamed and irritated by food groups that they have been exposed to via their mother's milk or in their formula milk. In this time, you may still see some symptoms but you should notice an improvement in their obvious symptoms quite quickly, e.g. their silent reflux. Some babies will become a different baby overnight when you take out the food that their gut is reacting to (for example, oats), much the same as if they have an allergy and you take out the allergen itself. Other babies are more complex little creatures and need you to look at several food groups to get to the bottom of things.

Formula Feeding – The Milk Journey

A baby who is either combination fed or exclusively formula-fed is, in some ways, easier to troubleshoot as you just have one variable to contend with – their milk. Most babies will start off on a straightforward first milk, by whichever brand parents have chosen to use. If baby is reacting to this milk by showing the symptoms we have identified, then the next steps to be taken are to move to different milk options.

Partially Hydrolysed Milks

Firstly, move from number one milk to a comfort milk. Most formula brands offer a 'comfort' milk version of their formula. This type of formula is partially hydrolysed, which means it is partly broken down (by up to 50 per cent) so that both the milk protein and the lactose in the milk is much reduced and therefore easier to digest. I often see significant improvements in babies on full formula diets who go from normal formula to comfort milk, therefore it is a good option for those babies struggling with what we might call dairy overload but who do not have a full allergy to cow's milk.

If baby goes on to comfort milk and appears to be doing much better, then you can stick with comfort milk. However, a trend we often see is that they can sometimes appear to be doing well, but then go backwards after around five to seven days on this milk, with their symptoms returning. We understand this to be the body getting used to having less dairy for a short while, so finding it easier, but the comfort milk is not enough to make them fully comfortable. Comfort milk can also contain additional ingredients so the impact of less dairy could be counteracted by the extra component that baby needs to learn to break down – look out for maltodextrin and added starch that can be difficult for baby to digest. At this stage you might then move to the next stage milk.

Fully Hydrolysed Milks

If your baby's symptoms are not changed by comfort milk, or you want to choose to skip the comfort milk stage in order to make baby more comfortable more quickly, then the next option to try would be a hydrolysed milk. These milks are not available off the shelf (in the UK) but can be purchased via a pharmacy or requested on prescription. This type of formula is made from dairy, but the protein in the milk is fully broken down. This can help with digestion as well as improve any immune response that the body is having to the milk in the case of a milk allergy.

A baby who reacts to both normal and comfort formula may be much better on a hydrolysed formula. It is quite common for symptoms to improve with these milks. As with the comfort milk, it can be usual to see a short-term improvement with symptoms then going backwards after around one week or so. If this is the case, it is worth thinking about whether, even though the milk is broken down, the dairy it is made from is still enough to be triggering reactions for your baby. In this case, the next step would be to try an amino acid-based milk, which is completely dairy free.

Amino Acid-Based Formula

The final stage for a baby when it comes to formula milk is a completely dairy-free version, made from amino acid-based components. Amino acids are the most basic version of proteins. These milks are generally plant-based, from ingredients such as coconut, corn, vegetable oil and sunflower oil. These amino acids are broken down so that the body does not recognise them as protein, creating an allergenic response. Hence, amino acid formula milks are classed as hypoallergenic.

These milks are expensive and difficult to get on prescription for that exact reason. On occasion, I have clients who have purchased the milk themselves to see if symptoms improve before then asking for it on prescription, as for a baby showing no obvious milk allergy symptoms, they are often not considered an option by many doctors, making it hard for parents to help their baby become more comfortable. Should a baby do well on that milk, this can be reported to their doctor who can then refer on accordingly.

With all of the above milks, it is important not to chop and change on a regular basis. It can feel difficult to see it through, but sometimes there will be a temporary increase in symptoms before improvement. Usually, unless baby is having an adverse reaction to a formula, take a minimum of five days to a week before deciding whether the new formula is indeed working for baby or not. Once you have found a formula that does sit better in their gut, then it will also take time for the inflammation in the gut to reduce too. This is why symptoms often do not go away completely. While some babies do have this overnight change in their entire wellbeing and personality, others take a little longer.

Alongside the formula milk changes, it is important to keep checking they are feeding optimally from the bottle itself. This is why air intake and checking for tongue ties and oral tension need to happen alongside any dietary changes. When a baby takes in air while feeding, this in itself can aggravate the gut and, therefore, even if on the right milk, there could still be some level of sensitivity until the reduction of air occurs.

Case Study: Baby Sienna, 3 months

Sienna was a healthy and thriving little girl who was struggling with short naps but otherwise seemingly feeding and sleeping well. She was a formula-fed baby, whose only other sign of possible milk sensitivity was her frequent and explosive pooing. Sienna's parents had been told that this was all normal, and that babies do just do short naps. When we spoke on our first call, we adapted some of Sienna's awake windows to ensure that she was neither over- or undertired. Sienna was already able to fall asleep on her own, so we had two options: to either accept her short naps as normal and see how these went as she got older or to explore her tummy and regular pooing by reducing the total dairy content of her formula. We moved her from a number one milk to a comfort milk (available off the shelf) and within two days Sienna was taking longer day time naps and her nappies were more formed. The small but significant reduction in dairy in her diet had created the ability to stay asleep for longer, and for her bowels to be happier too.

Pushing for Support

As we have explored, so often a baby's symptoms will be normalised or dismissed when there are no full-blown allergy symptoms. This can be frustrating and make you feel as though your instinct as a parent is not being taken seriously. While the healthcare system in the UK is free and brilliant in so many ways, there is a lack of understanding about the importance of gut health and why it would be much more beneficial to baby to reduce the inflammation and build the gut over just letting baby 'grow out of it'. We are years away from this being the case, so in the meantime you will need to push hard for what you feel is the right path for your baby. This means reading up and sometimes making the suggestion on behalf of your baby, rather than waiting for it to be offered. You can also purchase all of these formula milks over the counter, although they are expensive. An alternative step would be to go to a private paediatrician to discuss your concerns, as they are generally more likely to take milder symptoms more seriously and trial the various formula milks with you. Remember that you know your baby best. If you feel that their gut is not happy, then you are probably right.

Breastfeeding – The Exclusion Diet Journey

While there seems to be a level of understanding that cow's milk protein in formula milk can be something a baby reacts to, with breastfeeding there is unfortunately even less of a consensus around a baby's reaction to their mother's milk. In fact, many lactation consultants, health visitors and doctors I have come across in my time working with babies have been completely dismissive of this being relevant. There are vastly differing opinions on what foods and how much of these pass over into breastmilk, with little information available on what to do if you believe this to be the case for you and your baby.

One of the reasons that it is so difficult to be taken seriously and get the right help and support is because this is an area that is difficult to research. Each and every mother has a completely different metabolic rate for breaking down foods. Other variables will include how much food passes from the gut into the mother's milk, how much is transferred over to baby, and how quickly that happens – it could be a difference of hours or a day or more. Studies have also tracked some proteins that transfer across to milk in some mothers, but not for others.

Noticing Food Reaction Patterns

Research in this area remains thin on the ground so we have to work with each mother and baby individually to assess a pattern. One of the most common ways of doing this is the use of a food diary to keep a record about feeding and symptoms; however these are not conclusive in themselves. From experience, foods can take anything from 4–6 to 48+ hours to show up as a reaction in baby. This means that it can be hard to determine whether the reflux flare-up, broken sleep or rash is related to your previous breakfast, lunch or dinner. A mother's instinct counts for a lot though and by keeping a diary, you usually see at least some sort of a pattern, and often a starting point to be able to identify a trigger food.

Once a trigger food has been identified, the next step would be to cut that food group out and see how baby reacts. This should be done for at least 4–5 days, although some professionals suggest it can take weeks for a food protein to be totally out of the system. In my experience, the vast majority of parents will see a change within days, so there is no need to give up major food groups for up to six weeks as per some of the guidance. In fact, recent research from Free to Feed confirms that proteins leave the milk within days rather than weeks.

The Full Elimination Diet

It is possible that a baby can be reactive to not just one but multiple food groups – for example, dairy, oats and legumes – through their mother's milk. These babies often need time for their gut to calm and inflammation to reduce and heal before then being exposed to these foods again. If a baby is reactive to foods in their early months, it is important to note that it does not necessarily mean they will go on to have multiple allergies later in life and many babies will outgrow these within the first year. For most, this is more of a short-term problem relating to gut health that can be fairly easily changed by giving baby the right kind of foods to digest. In time, the reintroduction of certain food groups once the gut is balanced and healed might be possible as the gut is repopulated and repaired.

A full elimination diet is one in which you strip back the majority of foods that are known to cause a problem. There are various lists of top allergenic foods, FODMAP foods, foods that are harder to digest, and reflux-inducing foods, however there is no one set list that is officially used and the top allergens will differ from the top foods that babies struggle to digest, making it even harder to then navigate. These lists tend to differ depending on where you look. For my clients specifically, we tend to use the following list, in order of how much of a reaction we see, and always ensure that they follow up with a dietician to ensure that they are getting the correct support needed for maintaining their health and milk supply at the same time.

✧ Dairy – cheese, yoghurt, milk and any foods that contain milk in the ingredients

✧ Soy – edamame beans, soy sauce (used as a preservative in many foods, which can make it quite hard to avoid, especially in more processed foods)

✧ Eggs – both on their own but also cooked egg in cakes and baked goods

✧ Gluten – this is a hard one as busy parents often rely on things like bread and pasta

✧ Legumes – always a surprise with clients, but one that is hugely effective when cut out; this includes lentils, peas, chick-peas and beans as well as peanuts

✧ Grains – such as oats, corn and rice but this is a large group of foods which can make things very difficult

✧ Nuts – these are actually usually easier to navigate now as nuts have clear labelling due to nut allergies

It goes without saying that this list can be overwhelming. As a mummy to three babies who all had multiple food allergies and sensitivities, I have done this diet three times for varying amounts of time and the first time with my first baby was hard. I lasted a few months and then opted to move him on to an amino acid-based formula as I couldn't work out how to live, work and look after a baby while eating this way. The third time around though, it became second nature to me having practised twice before. In a world where we are now trying to avoid ultra-processed foods, it means you end up eating fresh foods much of the time, with less of an emphasis on snacking to get you by. This is, of course, much easier said than done when trying to look after a newborn and a family, which is why the elimination diet is not for everyone and you should consider all factors when deciding to give it a try – including your physical and mental health too.

Foods that tend to trigger less reaction for the majority of babies, and therefore are considered safe foods in this short period, include lamb, turkey, pork, courgette, olives, avocado, banana, carrots, butternut squash, salad, peppers, cauliflower and broccoli. These are more simple foods, but this diet is not designed for you to stay on for too long. In fact, after the initial period of five days, you should start adding foods back in slowly and monitoring your baby's reactions. While it is hard to find much information on exclusion diets online or even from your doctor, the Free to Feed organisation have leading research in this field and we will often pass clients on to them should we establish that a mother is needing to go on to an elimination diet, to ensure that they get the correct help and support. Not only that, but the company are soon to launch an allergy test strip for mothers to actually test their milk to see which foods are crossing over to baby, which could be a life-saver for so many other parents in the future.

The elimination diet is designed to be super-short term, as within about five days of eating basic foods, you should see a significant improvement in your baby's symptoms. If you do not, and you have done the elimination successfully, while there is a small chance that there is another food you need to take out, it is more likely that there is another cause for your baby's symptoms. This is why I would always recommend a full oral/mouth assessment before moving on to an exclusion diet.

Advantages

✧ A quick way of getting to the bottom of your baby's discomfort, rather than a long and drawn-out process

✧ Reduces the need to medicate baby if you can find the root cause of their symptoms

✧ Less need to do long periods of one food group (e.g. removing dairy if it is not the trigger)

Disadvantages

✧ Elimination diets take out nutrients, therefore you need to supplement and work out ways to put those back into your diet

✧ These diets can be mentally challenging, especially when out and about

✧ You need to ensure you are still eating plenty of calories, to avoid milk supply reducing

Lactose Intolerance and Overload

It is worth noting the impact of lactose on your baby's gut. Their gut can be affected by an excess of lactose, which generally causes symptoms such as tummy discomfort, green poo, wind and irritation of the stomach and gut. (Complete lactose intolerance itself is very rare, with far fewer babies suffering from this.) Lactose overload or intolerance is often mistaken for a milk intolerance and, in my experience, can be confusing for parents to understand. There are two main parts of milk that we need to know about – the milk protein itself and then the lactose. The lactose is the sugar part of the milk, and too much of this can cause baby issues if they're not able to break it down.

With formula milk, lactose can be reduced by giving baby a lactose-free milk, or by adding Colief drops to milk in order to break down some of the lactose for your baby first. Colief, or similar colic drops, contains an enzyme helping to break down the lactose for baby, so that it causes them fewer issues. While this can help reduce some of their bottom end symptoms, it will not alleviate any reflux symptoms, as it is the protein in the milk that triggers most of the reflux symptoms, rather than the lactose. What this means is that baby needs not a lactose-free milk but what is called a hydrolysed milk in order to be fully comfortable.

For breastfed babies, Colief drops can also be used to lower the lactose level of breast milk if baby is suffering from lactose over-load. This can happen for a variety of reasons, such as:

✧ An oversupply of breastmilk

✧ Baby taking in too much foremilk by swapping breasts too quickly and not emptying one side first

✧ A shallow latch (possible tongue tie) as baby struggles to effectively drain the breast and therefore survives on mostly the thinner foremilk

✧ A baby who simply feeds too often and therefore takes little and often

If you feel your baby is struggling with lactose overload symptoms alongside or instead of symptoms of reflux, then it would be worth addressing the possible root cause of this, such as changing up the way in which you feed your baby, or considering an oral assessment if their latch is shallow and they do not seem to be fully satisfied by feeds. Block-feeding can be useful; it's a method of breastfeeding that helps baby get to the hindmilk by offering only one breast per feed, and for a set period of time – for example three hours. If baby feeds again before three hours, then the same side is offered to ensure that they don't just take the more watery foremilk from the new breast, but get to the hindmilk on the breast that has recently been fed from. This should be done carefully as it can reduce supply, and theories on hind and foremilk and how long they are in milk for are mixed. As ever, it is about doing what works for your feeding journey and your baby.

I truly believe the information in this chapter is crucial to being able to work out your baby's comfort levels and to have this information accessible will be life-changing for so many parents. As a society, we are slowly recognising that our modern-day diets, including farmed dairy and processed foods, are causing havoc with our gut health. The knock-on impact is on our babies' guts.

Nevertheless, while I am passionate that this is useful information, I must stress that I am not a nutritionist and therefore should you find that your baby is better off without you eating multiple food groups, please do consider seeking outside support from a professional who is able to work with you to ensure that your body is getting what it needs, both for your own and for your baby's health.

Summary

✧ A baby's immature gut can be at the root cause of many challenges in the first few months, including their feeding, sleep and overall comfort levels.

✧ Certain variables can impact how strong a baby's gut is, including their birth, antibiotic exposure, the mother's gut and baby's gestational age.

✧ Not all formula milks are the same and there are off-the-shelf milk options, including more specialist milks, which can be discussed and trialled by parents.

✧ Food can pass through breastmilk to your baby, who may respond to this milk by being unsettled, showing allergy or intolerance symptoms and/or having broken sleep.

✧ Exclusion diets are an option but should not be undertaken lightly, as they can have knock-on consequences on a mother's physical and mental health.

✧ Your baby's gut is at the centre of their overall wellbeing, but it can be hard to find the right help and support as research into gut health is fairly new in the baby world, with much to learn for many of us, including medical professionals.

11

Shaping Sleep Slowly From 6 Weeks

It is often around about the 6-week mark that new parents start to become more tired and are ready for a little more predictability to their days. Post-birth hormones are settling down, the excitement of baby's arrival has passed and, most noticeably, the lack of sleep starts to take its toll. Fortunately, this is the perfect time to begin implementing some slow and steady sleep strategies. I find many parents are ready to be doing a little more than just surviving the newborn period by this age and if baby is comfortable and feeding is going well, sleep should start falling into place more easily. If you are reading this still in your newborn bubble, do not worry. There is no rush to start any of the upcoming sleep tips; sleep can be shaped whenever you are ready. As ever, lean into your wonderful gut feeling and see what it has to tell you about where you are at. You can come back to this chapter at 8 weeks, 12 weeks, or later on when you are out of the fourth trimester, because all of these ideas apply to babies of all ages.

As your baby reaches the 6-week mark, you will likely notice that they begin to become much more alert and suddenly seem to have grown a lot. They are starting to uncurl from their newborn foetal position and generally appear to be more vocal. At six weeks they are often growing fast and feeding is settling down. With all ages of babies, feeding should always be going well before starting to focus on tackling sleep. A baby who is feeding well has the potential to sleep well, which is why we have covered not just feeding but also factors affecting your baby and their comfort levels in the previous chapters. Sleep simply does not happen if your baby is not feeling comfortable and at ease.

Shaping Sleep: Step One – Regulating Their Body Clock

You will likely be very aware that your baby did not really have any idea about the difference between day and night when they were first born. In fact, babies often have their day and nights mixed up because of their sleep patterns in the womb. Yes, that is right – babies do sleep in the womb and research has found that they develop stages of sleep just as we do in the outside world. Your baby was likely used to being walked around in the womb during the day time when you were busy which likely meant that they slept for a lot of the 'day'. When you then sat down in the evening, chances are they were more lively and so, therefore, their evening and often nights too may have been quite wakeful. This is something that many parents notice and want to tackle once they are out of the other side of those first precious weeks.

Your baby's 'circadian rhythm' is not fully developed until somewhere between two and four months of age. Their circadian rhythm is essentially their body clock, helping them understand when it is time to wake up, and when it is time to go to sleep. This rhythm occurs over a 24-hour period, and can help regulate not only sleep patterns, but feeding, hormones and temperature regulation too. For this reason, it is pretty useful for us to start working on this from fairly early on, as it will have a direct impact on how sleep goes during the night time.

Some will argue that there is no point in starting a routine or working on sleep for the first 3–4 months of a baby's life, until their circadian rhythm has fully developed, but when we understand how the circadian rhythm is influenced, we can see exactly why it is worth putting in the ground work early on. Giving baby signs that their day time begins at 7am, for example, and their night time starts at 7, 8 or 9pm (more on this later), means that their body clock will start to regulate, which will make going down for sleep easier.

Babies love predictability as much as parents do. Therefore, our first step in helping shape sleep for our baby is to start waking them at the same time each day. Waking your baby at the same time every day may sound simple, but imagine a bad night and then still having to get up at a set time. It feels hard, doesn't it? This is the reason you need to be ready to start implementing sleep-shaping. If you have other children who are already awake bright and early, then without even meaning to, your baby's body clock will likely already be starting to sync with theirs. When you do wake your baby up, ensure that there is movement and sound, with some natural light being an important key component of this. Rather than just picking them up and snuggling them back off to sleep, ideally you will open the curtains, talk to them in a happy and 'day time' tone and go about your day.

Deciding on the time to wake your baby is entirely up to you. In the UK, many parents favour a 7am wake-up time. This seems to sit alongside parents' work commitments, and doesn't feel too early. Others might decide to have an 8am wake-up time, or a 6am wake-up. The time you choose should work for your family and your family only. Bear in mind that whatever time you choose, eventually I would suggest aiming for a bedtime 12 hours later from that wake-up time. So if you are choosing to start your day at 7am, then a 7pm bedtime will likely follow in the coming months; an 8am wake-up time means an 8pm bedtime, and so on. Think then about what works for both parents, and whether you have to factor in getting home from work, commitments to other children, when you eat and generally what feels right to you and your family. By waking up your baby at the same time each day, you will see that everything else that happens in their day will start to regulate and become a little more predictable. This is the magic of the circadian rhythm in action.

Shaping Sleep: Step Two – Show Baby the Difference

Once you have decided on your get-up time for the day, you will be able to start helping baby to understand the difference between day time and night time. This can be done by keeping day times really interactive and fun, and night times calm and quiet. Given newborn babies are up a lot in the night time, you might feel the need to keep yourself awake during night feeds. While some level of interaction with a tablet or book may keep you from falling asleep during night feeds, I recommend keeping light and noise levels to a minimum during baby's night time. We know that light levels have a direct impact on our ability to sleep and produce melatonin, which baby will start doing within their first 3–4 months of age. I would imagine we are all in agreement that the production of the sleepy hormone melatonin, which helps sleep happen, is best kept for night time.

During the night time, night lights or feeding lamps that have an orange or amber glow, rather than bright white or blue light, are helpful. Phones are notoriously bad at emitting the wrong kind of light, but it is entirely your choice as to whether or not you use your phone for night feeds. Perhaps sorting a podcast and then leaving your phone to the side could be an option, keeping you company and awake, but not potentially disturbing your ability to get back to sleep.

As well as keeping night times quiet, calm and dark, we must also make sure that day time means day time. Lots of activity, noise and the general chaos of your days with a baby will help. Your baby's body clock is also fed by natural light, so getting outside in the open air at least once a day would be really helpful. There is some confusion around whether or not putting a baby into a dark room for day time naps can interrupt or confuse their body clocks – and my suggestion to clients is always the same. If your baby is happy napping in the light (which they often are until six weeks of age or so), then great; don't worry about closing the blinds or curtains. However, if your baby struggles to settle for naps and is a light sleeper, then darkness can be really useful. In situations where babies nap in darker rooms, I have never yet found a baby who becomes confused by it. If anything, they are often just even better nappers because of it. (There is more to come on daytime naps very shortly.)

Shaping Sleep: Step Three – Pick a Bedtime

Like picking a wake-up time to start your day, selecting a bedtime for your baby is a good way of letting their body clock know that sleep is on its way. In the first few months, it will likely suit both you as a family and your baby that their bedtime is later. Babies often like to tank up on milk in the evenings which means feeding more frequently. Also, due to often being quite active in the evenings during your pregnancy, their pattern is probably to stay awake in the evenings too. Many families will enjoy this pattern, especially in a two-parent family with one parent who returns home from work having not seen their baby all day. Evening cuddles and hanging out together can be a lovely time, so there is no rush to start an earlier bedtime for your baby until you feel ready to do so.

At the same time, there are many families who already have children going to bed earlier in the evening so it makes total sense to put baby down around the same time. Choosing an earlier bedtime can also mean time to have a bath, or dinner and get some other bits done yourself, especially if you are finding having a new baby overwhelming. There really is no right time to do this, but from experience in troubleshooting sleep, I find that implementing an earlier bedtime by around 3–4 months tends to give the smoothest transition into sleep falling into place.

Again, with deciding a bedtime, it is crucial that you fit your baby's bedtime to your day time schedule. This should take into consideration the following:

✧ Do you have a partner who gets home from work in the evening? What time? Do they want to be able to see your baby before bed? If so, for how long? Are they happy for baby to be in bed before they get home?

✧ Have you got other children who already have a bedtime routine? If so, what time do they go to sleep? Will you be better off having the same bedtime or staggering it?

✧ Do you have any family traditions like eating dinner as a family? Will this affect when baby goes down to bed? Will they be eating with you once they start weaning?

Once you have decided that your baby's bedtime will be at a set time (let's say 7pm now, for ease of explaining), then one of the biggest dilemmas in baby sleep can be how to bring bedtime earlier once you have been enjoying those late night newborn cuddles. There are two potential ways to introduce an early bedtime for a new baby:

1. Just get stuck in and start with a 7pm bedtime from whenever you are ready. It may take a few days to a week for your baby to get used to their new bedtime, but if you stick at it and stay consistent with them being in a darkened room from your bedtime onwards, their body clock will soon adapt.

2. Move bedtime a little earlier over a number of weeks. This might be 9pm to start with, and then 8.30pm for another few days, with bedtime shifting by half an hour or so every 4–5 days. Doing it this way is a longer process but can feel less overwhelming than just starting with what feels like a much earlier bedtime.

I have used both options with families. Your baby will also naturally start to show you signs of tiredness and wanting to go down earlier in the evening as they get older. This often ties in with their melatonin production increasing as their circadian rhythm develops, meaning that they actually want to go down earlier too. Remember that, as with all of the sleep advice in this book, baby has to be fully comfortable otherwise sleep simply will not happen. For this reason, if you have been attempting an earlier bedtime for a while and are just not getting anywhere, then I recommend re-visiting previous chapters on wind, reflux and oral tension to assess whether anything else is coming up for your baby.

Heidi's Journey

With my first and my second child, I was keen to get
a routine established and started putting them into a
bedtime routine in the evenings from around 6 weeks of
age. This worked for me at the time and I was keen to still
find time for aspects of my life (work life, social life and
my marriage), so my evenings were precious to do those
things I still wanted to do. With my third baby, I have
known that she is my last baby but I was also trying to fit
in bed and bath time for two other children. Getting them
all down to bed for 7pm felt like too much of a hurdle,
especially as I did bedtime solo every evening during the
week. For this reason, I didn't introduce an earlier bedtime for my little girl until she was closer to 14 weeks. This
worked for us and shows the power in doing what you
feel fits your family best. Every baby and family set-up is
uniquely different.

Shaping Sleep: Step Four – Introduction of a Bedtime Routine

Once you have decided what time baby will be going to bed, this
is when the real fun begins – your bedtime routine! The science
of what works and doesn't work for baby sleep can be contradic-
tory and confusing at times, but there is no disagreement in the
fact that a bedtime routine can be the key component of a baby's
sleep. Multiple research studies have shown that when a child has

a bedtime routine, they are more likely to sleep better compared to those without. We have already explored setting up a consistent time to go to bed, so the next step is to add in the wind-down routine that will go on to serve you and your family's sleep for years to come.

Case Study: Baby Emma, aged 8 weeks

Emma's parents were first-time parents and were dealing with multiple hours of evening crying that had been branded as colic by various health professionals. They came to me when their relationship had started to struggle, with Dad working late and Mum having to take on the majority of these colicky evenings. We talked through Emma's day time routine and her feeding; she seemed to be thriving in all other areas but come the evenings would be inconsolable. Emma was seemingly overstimulated by the time that evening came around, so we discussed bringing her bedtime forwards to see if she settled more easily and it reduced the crying. Over a period of a week, we worked to move bedtime from 10pm to closer to 7pm. Emma's crying disappeared within a number of days and she was happily going down after a feed, without the hours of crying she had previously experienced. This was a classic case of an overtired baby, who was asking for an earlier bedtime before her parents had thought to implement it.

A bedtime routine is the simple sequence of steps and events that lead to your baby being able to be put down to sleep calmly, with them knowing that sleep is coming next. It becomes an essential part of your evenings as baby gets older, and is a sleep tool that can be used wherever you are. Not only this, but another caregiver can implement a bedtime routine for your baby, meaning that baby feels more secure when left with someone else as they will recognise the steps that are moving them towards falling asleep.

When your baby is only a few months old, this routine will be on the shorter side. If you include their feed, it could be as long as an hour but without their feed possibly only 15–20 minutes. It certainly does not have to be complex, as long as it is repeated in roughly the same way each evening. The introduction of a bedtime routine also gives you and your baby a chance to relax, unwind and spend some loving time together, away from the distractions of everything else. It can become a very sacred and special time for both parents and baby too.

The steps of your bedtime routine may look something like:

✧ A bath or a mini massage and changing into night clothes – babies do not need to be bathed every night and those with more sensitive skin may benefit from bigger gaps between their baths. For other families, it can be an important part of the routine. If opting to not do a bath every day, a simple baby massage routine or some baby yoga movements might be a nice activity to introduce. Touch helps release oxytocin, an important hormone in keeping baby feeling nice and relaxed.

✧ The last feed of the day – at only a few months of age, your baby will still need to feed directly before they go to bed and this is often a time when they are still cluster feeding too. For this reason, you may opt for a feed before their bath or massage, and then another one after too. We will explore feeding to sleep later on and the decision about whether to do this in the evenings or not.

✧ A story or two, so baby has time to sit up and wind after their feed. It may seem strange to consider reading a book for such a young baby, but reading to your baby is actually one of the best activities you can do. Talking to them, and showing them black and white story books can be a lovely connection time and as they get older they will start to become more and more interested.

✧ Cuddles and songs – the very last part of your bedtime routine. Giving your baby cuddles, singing to them, and winding them during this, is a lovely pre-requisite to sleep. This is a special time when they may well just fall asleep on you. There is no need to have your baby awake when they go down, unless you are purposefully working towards settling ability, which we explore in Chapter 15.

Building a short sequence of events that becomes predictable to your baby can be a wonderful way of helping sleep on its way to becoming more established. Bedtime routines are one of the most research-backed sleep strategies, so starting early and finding a routine that works for your baby is going to be a great building block for future sleep.

Summary

✧ Babies can be born with their days and nights back to front. Waking baby at the same time each day can start to help set their internal rhythm, which signals to them when day and night time begin and end.

✧ Creating calm and dark night settings alongside more wakeful, noisier day times, can help show baby the difference between day and night time, and support their body clocks to develop.

✧ A baby's bedtime can be anytime from early evening through to later in the night when you go to bed. As baby gets bigger, you will likely find that they will show signs of wanting to go down earlier.

✧ Most parents in the UK choose a bedtime of 7pm, but the time can be chosen to best fit your family's needs.

✧ Setting up a bedtime routine with a simple sequence of steps before baby falls to sleep in the evening can positively impact their sleep moving forwards.

12

Setting Up a Routine and Awake Windows

The word 'routine' often fills many parents with dread, when it does not need to. The culprit is usually outdated baby care books asking parents to stick to exact schedules with a less than soft approach should they wander outside the lines of the page. Let's be honest, we all have that one friend who has to be home between 12pm and 2pm for their baby's nap time, no matter what the weather and what plans were made. The word 'routine' can feel somewhat restrictive. I get it, and it makes total sense that lots of parents are now sceptical of strict routines.

Baby care has changed significantly over the last ten or more years. When I first trained as a maternity nurse, it was all we knew and loved. Most clients wanted a set routine to work towards, with some of the biggest names in the baby care industry becoming famous for their no-nonsense, 'get baby sleeping through the night by a few months of age' approach. Life has moved on and changed since then though, and parents are now opting for more flexible routines that work alongside their baby and their lifestyle. In my own practice as a baby sleep coach, I have also developed and adapted my work alongside new science and research into child development and been able to carve my own path in what I feel works best for young families with new babies. For this reason, I now advocate what we call a 'flexible routine'.

This approach to baby care uses the principles of a routine that we know and love – doing the same things at the same time each day so that baby comes to understand what is going to happen and responds more easily, and mixes that with greater flexibility to allow parents to get out and about and enjoy being social with their baby. Since we now live mostly without close family members nearby to turn to for support, if we need to pop out to an appointment then our babies have to follow. We need flexibility within our days as we juggle the many demands of parenting alongside running a home, being social and everything else that modern-day life includes. At the same time, we also, more often than not, crave structure, understanding that babies do thrive in patterns, better known as a routine.

Choosing a Routine to Suit You

The million-dollar question that parents often ask me when they have a baby: when to start a routine? Some parents crave a routine from as early as a few weeks, others would prefer not to have a routine at all. I will hazard a guess that if you are reading a baby care book, then you are likely more in the camp of wanting a little more structure to your days. This can be for many reasons – each individual family has very different wants and needs. I do not advocate one approach that fits all, because that doesn't exist. In this chapter, I will introduce you to several routine options that I have used over the last ten years of my career and you can choose which type of approach suits your family best.

When to introduce a routine for your baby remains subjective; there is no clear-cut answer. If you have a 6-week-old and are a big routine fan, then you can absolutely introduce a day time routine should you wish to. This assumes that your baby is feeding well and comfortable, which is key for your baby in being able to sleep well, have longer naps, and therefore get into a routine. My preferred approach is to have a flexible routine in place by around 12 weeks of age, as I believe this to be helpful in shaping your baby's naps and nights, but also gives you as parents a sense of being in control of your days. This is something that I believe has a huge impact on maternal mental health.

For my clients, a routine gives them a sense of understanding their baby. Rather than forcing something on to their baby, they come to understand and see that actually by having rough ideas of when their baby sleeps or feeds, they appreciate and can recognise their baby's cues and cries more easily, not less so. Today, social media sleep accounts have caused a huge stir and divide in the baby sleep world, and the idea that you are forcing your baby into a pattern that doesn't suit them is often what a 'routine' is seen to be. From my work and significant baby care experience, this couldn't be further from the truth. My routines are all explained below, and it is entirely up to you as a parent to work out the sort of routine you would like.

Awake Windows – the Core Component of Routines

Your baby has a unique time that they can stay awake for before they then get tired again. This short period of time is their 'awake window'. Awake windows are a newer concept in the baby sleep world, developed off the back of more understanding of baby sleep, and the way sleep works. As we spend time awake, adenosine, a chemical in the brain that makes us feel sleepy, builds up, prompting the need to go to sleep. Babies have much shorter awake windows than we do as adults, hence the need for many more naps across their day time.

Although awake windows can be explained with the science of sleep, they are not a scientifically researched area of sleep so they are hugely open to interpretation. One sleep coach's awake window table will differ to that of another, simply because they are based on the individual sleep coach's experience of working with clients. You will also find that some sleep coaches are very dismissive of awake windows altogether – just to confuse you!

In the last few years, I have found awake windows to be extremely useful for working with smaller babies and I am a big fan of them. When using older baby care books, I can see now that the awake windows, or time between naps as it was phrased back then, was far too long. Through putting these routines into practice for so many babies, I began to find my own preferred nap timings and awake windows. The awake windows you see overleaf now apply to over 90 per cent of the babies that I work with. They are a brilliant starting point for working out the sweet spot at which your baby both settles best and sleeps for the longest afterwards.

An awake window allows you to predict when your baby will next need to go down for a nap, or down for the evening, by understanding the total time for which they can be awake. Once they reach the end of their awake window, you get them to sleep ideally. This will not always happen on the dot, but gives you a rough guide to help you spot when your baby needs to go down to sleep. On my online courses, I recently surveyed 4,000 parents and 84 per cent of them said that learning about their baby's awake windows had positively contributed to better sleep for their baby.

During the fourth trimester, the slight challenge with using awake windows is your baby's inability to stay awake for long, combined with their feeds, taking a long time particularly if there are feeding challenges too. These two things combined can mean the awake window is hard to stick to in those early weeks, which is why I recommend using them sparingly in the early days. They are brilliant to be aware of, otherwise you may just assume that your newborn can stay awake for three hours at a time, but you certainly should not stress about them. Focusing on feeding is your number one priority in those early weeks and months, therefore if you find yourself going over the awake window on a regular basis, please do not worry. Use them as a guideline, not to make your life more difficult.

As a general rule of thumb, your baby's awake window will increase by 15 minutes with every month that they get older, looking similar to the below:

Age of Baby	Awake Window
1 month	45–60 minutes
2 months	1hr–1hr 15 minutes
3 months	1hr 15–30 minutes
4 months	1hr 30–45 minutes

Your baby's awake window will often need to be shorter than the average if:

✧ It is earlier in the day time – the first awake window of the day is usually shorter than the average for their age.

✧ Your baby is taking very short naps – if naps are broken or very short, they can be more tired sooner, therefore a reduced awake window will be needed.

✧ Nights are very broken – small babies wake often in the night but if your baby appears to be very unsettled, they will probably be more tired during the day time.

✧ Your baby is in discomfort – a baby who is uncomfortable and potentially in pain, for example with their tummy, may need shorter awake windows.

When starting out with awake windows, it may feel strange that your baby is going down to sleep so soon after waking up. It is quite normal to even receive comments from well-meaning family members, asking why your baby needs to sleep again so soon. Leaving your baby until you see signs of tiredness such as yawning, or getting agitated, usually means they are overtired. So trusting in the awake windows and seeing what happens would be your first step in making sleep happen for your baby. That said, all babies are of course different, so you may want to tweak them by 10–15 minutes each way if you feel they are not working for your baby. This is best done over a number of days, so that you can track a pattern and find the best awake window that works for your baby.

Choosing a Routine

Before you pick and choose which style of routine you would like to go for, it's important to recognise that just like any other changes you make with a baby, they can take time. Although it would be lovely, your baby will not wake up and know that you are planning a different sort of day for them, so try not to feel disheartened if things don't go to plan. I always advise clients to stay local for the first week of implementing a routine. In this time, you can of course go out and about for naps and so on, as we are not focusing on just cot naps in the fourth trimester. However, if you are using awake windows, you will probably find it easier to stay local or close to home to start with while you build your confidence.

Once a routine is established, then it is super easy to go out and about and adjust timings accordingly. I like to call out-and-about days 'off routine' days, where you go out with your baby and just enjoy being out, being social, and have a little adventure together with no set time to be home or worries about nap times. Although this idea might fill you with dread, there is nothing negative about having an 'off routine' day and, if anything, I highly recommend them. Maybe on these days, you use the sling for naps, or your baby does shorter pram naps. This is all totally ok, and having an off routine day is not going to ruin all of your hard work of establishing a routine in the first place.

Case Study: Joseph, aged 9 weeks

Little Joseph was a bonny blue-eyed baby, who was doing only 10–12-minute naps across the day time and feeding so frequently that when Mum contacted me, she was thinking of giving up breastfeeding. She couldn't understand how the babies from her antenatal class were all sleeping in their prams for naps, yet Joseph was awake most of the day. During our consultation, it turned out that Joseph was busy staying awake for 4–5 hours at a time during the day time, and seemed to be incredibly overtired. I worked with Mum to establish both a feeding and sleeping routine, which Jospeh took to almost immediately. By following the suggested awake times for his age, his naps went from 20 minutes to up to 2 hours, and he no longer needed to feed every hour as he was sleeping well and then taking bigger feeds as a consequence.

The Flexi Baby Routine

This is the most popular type of routine because it incorporates both a structure to the day, but allows for total flexibility as well. Not only that, but it flexes throughout the day time depending on what sort of day your baby is having. Some days may be a day of longer naps and on other days they might have more frequent and shorter naps, both being totally ok for your baby in the fourth trimester.

The flexi baby routine works around your baby's awake windows, which we have just learned. So for a 3-month-old, that would be an awake window of around 1 hour and 15–30 minutes. In a flexi routine, you will still choose a start time to your day, e.g. 7am, and start waking baby at the same time each day. From then onwards, the day will work by following baby's awake window, putting them down for naps at the end of their awake window, but with no exact timings to their day or nap times.

For a baby with an awake time of 1 hour and 30 minutes, this may look something like:

Baby wakes for the day at 7am
Feed/Playtime
Baby sleeps from 8.30am to 9.45am (nap time is however long baby wants.)
Feed/Playtime
Baby sleeps from 11.15am to 12pm (nap time is however long baby wants.)
Feed/Playtime

This pattern then repeats throughout the day time, with various nap lengths, but with the consistency of their awake window being the one variable that doesn't change. Unless of course their nap is very short, or they appear very tired, in which case you may choose to reduce your baby's awake window before the next nap. Once you then come to the evening, your baby's bedtime will change slightly each night depending on their awake time. If you have chosen a 7pm bedtime to aim for, but their awake window means that they are ready for bed at 6.30pm then that is totally fine. If the awake window ends later at 7.30pm, that is fine too. Although you have chosen your set bedtime, it does not matter if this changes each evening by half an hour or so either way.

As your baby's naps begin to regulate and become longer, you will find that this routine becomes more structured in that every day you will see patterns in always feeding around 10am, or always going down for a nap at around 11.30am, and so on. At this stage, many parents prefer to move towards a 'set' routine, the second option we have available.

The Set Timed Baby Routine

For those parents who like to know what they are doing at the same time each day and feel a sense of unease over not having full control of timings, then a set timed baby routine may be your preferred option. This routine is similar to more old-school baby care routines, yet we understand now that we do not need to be as wedded to the page as we perhaps once were. There is no 'fail' should your baby not stick to the timings, and it is certainly nothing you have done wrong.

This sort of routine is sometimes requested by clients, especially those who are handing over their babies early to go back to work, or to family members who just simply do not get the concept of awake windows. Sometimes it is easier to work to specific timings, and have a routine that works around set feed and sleep times, if that is your preference.

This tiny baby routine can be used as early as 6 weeks of age if you feel ready, and then the 3- and 4-month routines are also listed below.

Example Tiny Baby Routine	
7am	WAKE AND FEED Wake baby up, change nappy and offer a full feed. Encourage a nice big feed and wind well afterwards. Some awake time afterward – face-to-face interaction, play mat, cuddles etc. (Repeat at wake and feed time.)
8.15-10am	SLEEP
	WAKE AND FEED
11.15-1pm	SLEEP
	WAKE AND FEED
2.15-4pm	SLEEP
	WAKE AND FEED
5.15-6pm	SLEEP (Walk in pram/sling)
	OFFER SNACK/FEED Offer baby half of a normal feed – so half of a bottle or half of a normal boob – this mimics cluster feeding and helps tank them up for the night.
	BATH TIME AND MASSAGE
	FULL FEED Full evening feed. Baby is likely to be tired and ready for bed, so will feed sleepily. Encourage baby to take a full feed, waking them halfway if needs be and talking to them, to try and stop them drifting totally off to sleep. Use breast compressions to encourage milk flow if breastfeeding. This is a good time of day to do a bottle if you are happy to introduce.
7.30pm	BEDTIME FOR THE NIGHT

Example 3-Month Baby Routine	
7am	WAKE AND FEED Milk feed
	PLAY TIME
8.30-10am	SLEEP (1.5 HOURS) If baby wakes after 30-45 minutes, try extending the nap by any sort of contact or movement, OR your sleep shaping approach if using one.
	WAKE IF STILL SLEEPING
	FEED
	PLAY TIME
	TOP UP MILK FEED
11.30am- 1.30/2pm	SLEEP (UP TO 2 HOURS) Longer "lunch" sleep here, aiming for at least 2 sleep cycles. If baby wakes before 1hr 30 (e.g. after 30-34 minutes), you can try and encourage baby back to sleep by resettling them with either a feed, cuddle, rocking, or one of the sleep shaping approaches within the newborn sleep course – that is IF you want to encourage a longer nap.
	MILK FEED May need a quick nap or catch-up nap here if middle of the day sleep wasn't a long one – so a third nap of the day.
3.30/4pm	SLEEP (1 HOUR TO 1.5 HOURS) The last nap of the day is always best as a movement or contact nap – such as the sling, car, pram or on you. If baby sleeps as close to 5pm as possible, that helps ensure they are not overtired and can make 6.30-7pm bedtime.
	SNACK FEED
	BATH TIME
	BEDTIME FEED
6.30/7pm	ASLEEP If you are implementing an early bedtime, go with this. If baby is then staying up later, you may just do another cat nap here and then put baby to bed after another awake window (e.g. later evening).

Example 4-Month Baby Routine	
7am (ish)	WAKE AND FEED Milk feed
	AWAKE TIME
8.45-10am	SLEEP (45 MINUTES TO 1.5 HOURS) (You can try and extend nap if baby wakes and appears tired).
	FEED
	AWAKE TIME
	TOP UP MILK FEED
11.45am/ 12-2/2.30pm	SLEEP (1.5-2hrs+) As with morning nap, if baby wakes early after 30-45 minutes, try and extend the nap into a second cycle if possible.
	MILK FEED
	AWAKE TIME
3.45/4-5pm	SLEEP (45-60 minutes) Always wake baby by 5pm.
	SNACK FEED
	PLAYTIME AND BATH TIME
	FEED
	BEDTIME ROUTINE Story / song / sleeping bag / sleepy time sentence.
6.30/7pm	ASLEEP

Summary

✧ Introducing a routine is a personal choice and there is no set cut-off time to introduce one.

✧ Many parents choose to introduce a gentle routine somewhere around 6–12 weeks of age.

✧ Awake windows are the holy grail of baby sleep and can make a huge difference to a baby's ability to both sleep for longer chunks of time, as well as settle to sleep more easily.

✧ Routines can be either set time routines or based on awake windows, with an emphasis on flexibility as all babies have good and bad days.

13

Day Time Naps

Perhaps one of the biggest challenges in the newborn period is helping your baby to sleep during the day time. Once again, napping comes with many differing views about what is considered normal for a small baby. Day time naps can be an absolute godsend for a tired new parent. They allow you to recharge, sit down and rest, snooze, eat, shower, or perhaps to do something in the house or for yourself – a rare treat in those early and rather hazy newborn months. Day time naps are equally as important for your baby and by establishing happy, healthy nap time rituals, we can move towards long, restorative naps which form part of baby's ongoing routine for at least a couple of years.

Day Time Naps - What Is Normal?

As you will have gathered by now, I am not going to normalise short naps, or no naps at all, just because you have a newborn. Common yes, but normalising a baby who cannot be put down for a nap, or who struggles to stay asleep for a nap, is not helpful when that baby could be napping more easily, more comfortably and allowing a parent to have a much smoother, happier time of their journey into parenthood.

The normalisation of short and difficult naps has not only left many parents feeling like they aren't enjoying their baby, but it also then misses the many babies who could be much more rested. While I understand that the approach of accepting that some babies don't sleep well, and just rolling with it, might be useful to some parents, I am passionate about getting my knowledge and information out there when it comes to baby sleep. If you were to ask a maternity nurse whether babies are able to do longer naps when little, they'll mostly say yes. Many of the babies in their care likely sleep well during the day time as they understand babies and know how to make them comfortable and help them sleep well. Given an average parent of a newborn does not have experience of babies, it is sometimes easier to normalise baby behaviour than it is to understand or have the energy to work out what can be done to help baby's naps. That's where this chapter comes in....

As with all parenting debates, you will need to decide what feels right for you. You can choose to be happy with naps that are on the shorter side and always on you, and decide to roll with it until these become easier in the future as baby grows. There is nothing wrong with this approach as long as you feel your baby is happy; if so, then be confident in your decision. Or, you might want to move towards better day time naps for your baby for your own personal reasons – other siblings, mental health, work commitments and so on. This chapter is designed to support you to understand why your baby may not be napping so well, and what you can then do to help them. It may not be an easy or simple process, but with time, and a bit of a plan, I believe that every new baby is capable of having proper established long day time naps lasting more than 30–40 minutes.

Why Can't I Put My Baby Down?

This is the billion-dollar question to which if I had just one answer, I would be a very rich lady. I do have lots of answers though, and this is one of the main reasons why I wanted to write this book for you all. There are many different reasons and answers to this question, so we'll start from the top...

Firstly, it is entirely possible to have a baby who can be put down for naps, if that is what you want. New babies love to be close to their mothers and research tells us that contact naps and closeness are crucial for baby's development. I think it is essential to point out here that we are not denying babies of those lovely contact naps – they are to be celebrated and recommended to all new parents. They simply become a bigger challenge when your baby can't be put down at all, needing to be upright on you all of the time, which then starts to impact not only your everyday life, but also your wellbeing as a parent. Being underneath a baby three, four or five times a day for an extended period is sustainable for some, but not for everyone, particularly with some mothers having to return to work sooner, as well as the juggle of the care of other children too.

Reasons for Contact Napping

Aside from simply just wanting to be close to you, if we think about how our baby sleeps best in the day time then we can perhaps work out what could be going on for them. If your baby only sleeps on you, think about the position they are in and how that could have an impact on their comfort levels. For the majority of babies, this is the reason contact napping works so well. They often nap either totally upright, at an angle, or on their side. These positions help them feel more comfortable as they are not flat on their backs, which is when wind and reflux create an issue with their sleep. Since the advice is now to put our babies to sleep on their backs rather than on their tummies, the likelihood is that there are going to be more babies who struggle to settle this way. Babies who are placed on their tummy to sleep have been found to have deeper sleep and wake less easily through noise and movement, which is part of the reason why it is recommended for a baby to sleep on their back, also contributing to a reduced risk of SIDS occurring.

When a baby is on their side or laying on their stomach, they often experience less regurgitation and wind can be less of an issue. This is one of the key reasons why babies end up being held for their day time naps. It is simply positioning that makes it easier for them to nap on someone. Whilst some parents are totally relaxed and happy to do this, others can struggle mentally and need to be able to sort the wind and reflux issues before being successful at putting baby down.

Moving Away From Contact Naps

For the first couple of weeks, you will probably be soaking up the contact naps with your baby, as will your partner and maybe other family members too. Remember that skin-to-skin is an important part of bonding with baby and in building their gut microbiome. Contact naps are to be encouraged in those early months, and can continue right into a baby's toddler years – there is no set time when you need to stop doing them. In fact (letting you into a little secret!), you can do both. You can have a baby who is confidently able to be put down to sleep, as well as a baby who enjoys a contact nap on you. Do not be made to feel like you have to choose. Too many mothers sacrifice what little time they have to themselves because they believe that they have to contact nap to have an attached baby. It is simply not the case. Your baby is loved, well cared for and you are full of responsiveness to them. You should not feel bad about wanting to put your baby down whenever you need to in order to have some necessary respite.

When I first look at a baby who is not able to be put down, I start with the basics. We do not want to jump to any conclusions, as so often it is just simply a matter of not having tried. To get you started, have a think about the following:

✧ Have you considered your baby's awake window and tried to settle them down for a nap as they get to the end of it? A baby who is awake much longer than this is often much harder to get to sleep.

✧ Is your baby full and receiving enough milk to settle them? Snack feeding or taking in air can cause baby to feel more full, when they actually aren't. It is worth thinking about whether hunger could be playing a role.

✧ Have you tried swaddling your baby to help with their startle reflex? It is really normal for babies to fling their arms backwards and wake themselves up. By swaddling, you reduce the chance of this and they may settle better.

✧ Have you tried putting baby down on their side to start with, settling them with patting and then turning them over on to their back once settled? Babies often prefer to be settled on to their side, and then you can put them on to their back slowly, ready for sleep.

✧ Babies can feel unsafe if they are lowered head first into a cot, the natural way we would go to put baby down. Try putting their feet on to the mattress first, followed by the middle of the body and then their head. Doing it this way can stop waking and mean an easier transfer.

✧ Have you simply practised putting baby down with all of the above combined? Just attempt to put your baby down a few times consistently and you will often see progress.

Having reviewed all of these basics above, if your baby is still fighting being put down to sleep for their day time naps, then it is entirely possible that there is something else bothering them.

Heidi's Journey

At various times, all three of my babies struggled with shorter day time naps and I am not afraid to say that I struggled with them too. I am a committed and loving mother, but I also run a business and needed time to be able to speak to clients or get some work done. Thirty- to forty-minute naps just didn't cut it and I saw a direct correlation between nap length and how happy they were. The shorter naps we experienced were always at times when they were struggling more with their wind, reflux or food sensitivities. I knew that if they were comfortable, they would nap well. I learned to lean in and be ok with the days that shorter naps happened, knowing that there was always a reason. At the same time, I tackled the root cause of it as this felt like the right thing to do for my mental health as well as my babies too.

The range of different reasons are quite vast and all have been covered in detail within this book. Perhaps you skipped over those chapters with the assumption that your baby isn't being bothered by any wind, air intake, reflux or body tension. If this is the case, I would recommend you revisit these chapters and take a further deep dive into the reasons why babies find sleep so difficult. Your baby is not pre-programmed to never be put down. Of course they love their cuddles as much as we love cuddling them, but a baby who will not be put flat on their back is usually trying to communicate something to us.

Common Reasons for Day Nap Refusal

It is quite common for me to see a small baby who sleeps well during the night time, but struggles with day time naps. These are usually the babies who are feeding frequently in the day time. Therefore their tiny tummies are often overloaded and they may be experiencing uncomfortable symptoms alongside that. When their tummies are emptier during the night time, they often go for longer stretches of sleep. It feels counterintuitive but a baby with a sensitive gut or tummy will often sleep better and not worse. For this reason, I ask my clients not to rule out any underlying issues causing sleep challenges just on the basis that a baby sleeps well at night time.

The most obvious causes of a baby not being able to put down for their day time naps include:

✧ **Baby suffering from regurgitation or silent reflux.** This means that on their back they are uncomfortable and, even if put down, are woken easily by stomach acid and milk coming back up.

✦ **Baby having body tension** which means they physically are not comfortable in a sleeping position on their own. They prefer to be bundled up on you and, until this tension is released, they won't be put down at all.

✦ **Wind** which then causes baby to have tummy ache, bloating and to be uncomfortable. These babies often won't be put down at all.

✦ **A dysregulated nervous system** which often links into being in pain or a potential tongue tie. A baby who is not able to get into a relaxed state within their body will not be able to be put down.

✦ **A baby who is highly sensitive.** These babies need a lot of reassurance in order to sleep and therefore may not be able to go down on their own. These babies are often put into a category of being highly sensitive and that just being their personality, however we have learned in our gut module that those babies with high levels of separation anxiety are often also the ones who have gut challenges or underlying discomfort.

For all of these reasons I am happy to challenge the basic concept that babies just do not want to be put down, and that contact naps are normal. Your baby is communicating with you more than you think. The normalisation of everything babies do, from crying to not napping, is incredibly frustrating both for parents wishing for a smoother parenting experience, and for me as a professional. Having spent thousands of hours with other babies as well as three of my own, I hope this gives you confidence that you will be able to put your baby down should you wish to. It is a process and there is lots of leg work to do to find out the root cause for your baby,

but once you get there, you will soon see that there is another way
— you just need to find it.

Case Study: Baby Grace, aged 12 weeks

Grace was a three month old baby who had only ever napped for 30 minutes, aside from the first two weeks of her life when she was very sleepy. By 12 weeks of age, mum was becoming increasingly frustrated with her lack of ability to stay asleep, particularly with a toddler around too. Mum had already worked hard at helping Grace to fall asleep on her own and had tried adjusting her awake windows, so booked a call with me to try and troubleshoot on what was happening. During the call, I quicky pinpointed various signs of silent reflux that Grace was showing but her mother was not keen to assess for tongue tie or look into her diet, being a busy mum of two. Instead, Grace was given Gaviscon from the GP and on the first day she slept for two longer naps, and has been doing longer naps ever since. By getting Grace's silent reflux under control this way, her ability to nap more comfortably and for longer was then much improved. Mummy was glad to have reached out and with such subtle signs, would not have noticed otherwise.

Short or Broken Naps – a Problem?

You will likely have found that for the first few weeks your baby was fairly sleepy. During this time, your baby is getting used to the outside world and is still asleep a lot of the time. Parents are often led into a false sense of security, assuming that they have an easy baby who likes sleep! Then the end of the second week hits, where baby starts to wake up more, struggles to settle as easily, and also starts to take shorter naps too.

This is not every baby. There are plenty of babies that I worked for, including two of my own, who continued to do longer naps throughout the fourth trimester. Some babies are easier sleepers and will nap for up to a couple of hours. Lots of babies on the other hand, start to do shorter naps and they can get stuck on these shorter naps for a number of months, potentially even longer depending on the reason for those short naps. First of all, please know that your baby is capable of doing longer naps. They are not biologically unable, as why would other babies be able at the same age? They simply have a huge amount of variables that lead into being comfortable enough to do a longer nap.

Encouraging Longer Naps

Your baby's sleep cycle is developing as they grow. During the fourth trimester it is most noticeable during their nap times. If your baby has developed into a short napper, then it is most likely that you will be seeing naps of around 30–45 minutes. This is roughly one sleep cycle. You may see lots of naps that finish at the end of a sleep cycle, and some naps that go into a second or third sleep cycle, meaning the nap will be longer. There is nothing wrong with a one sleep cycle nap and for lots of parents any nap is a good nap.

However, for some babies, one cycle naps mean that they wake up tired and perhaps do not feed as easily, with a knock-on effect that the short nap causes more of a challenge to baby's overall wellbeing. Not only this, but so often it is parents who struggle with a short napper too. By the time baby gets to sleep, there is little time to rest and eat something before the whole wake, feed and sleep cycle starts again. This can be exhausting and has been a key component in the enjoyment of the baby days for many clients that I have worked for.

The length of your baby's nap is so often a clue as to whether anything is going on for them or not. A nap that lasts only 10–20 minutes as a one-off is never a concern. However, if baby is napping for super-short durations on a regular basis, this is a definite indicator that there is something physiological waking them up. If a baby is only able to stay asleep for tiny bursts of time, and cannot get into deep sleep, then there is usually some sort of discomfort. This is most likely linked to airways, their gut, body tension or their nervous system. If this sounds like your baby, then skip back to the chapters covering those topics to find out more.

If your baby's nap duration is between 30–45 minutes, then they could be reaching the end of a full cycle, so the brilliant news is that they can get into a full cycle of sleep. This length of nap may well work totally fine for you and your baby. That said, if your baby is waking up after one sleep cycle seemingly tired, or upset, then you may wish to think about attempting to lengthen their nap for them. More often than not, it is simply wind that wakes them. When a baby rouses into lighter sleep between cycles, if there is anything niggling away at them (for example a stuck burp), then they are much more likely to wake up. For this reason, focus a lot of your awake time attention on winding baby, as well as thinking about the root causes of their wind such as food sensitivities and air intake during feeding. If your baby ticks any of the boxes on the reflux checklist, then you will also want to have a think about whether this could be affecting them. A baby with reflux will often have shorter naps as when they stir between cycles, this is when acid can creep up and cause them to become uncomfortable. The adrenaline then produced by their body to counteract the discomfort causes them to appear wide awake. This is why so many babies are impossible to resettle back to sleep with short naps as the adrenaline is working against them being sleepy or needing more sleep.

Your checklist for baby having longer naps includes:

✧ Checking in on their awake window and tweaking it accordingly to help them settle and stay asleep for the longest amount of time

✧ Making sure they are feeding well

✧ Winding baby to minimise any wind waking them up

✧ Ensuring that baby has no reflux symptoms and, if they do, tackling the root cause of them head-on

✧ Watching that your baby is not mouth breathing and, if they are, getting to the bottom of this

✧ Looking out for other signs that your baby's gut is unhappy

✧ Ensuring that baby has no tension that is causing them to be more unsettled in their sleep

✧ Keeping an eye out for any other underlying medical issues that could potentially pose an issue to your baby's comfort levels

As we have explored, getting to the bottom of any possible wind or reflux issues can take some time. It is often not a matter of changing one variable and seeing a significant improvement. During this process, there is another factor to consider and that is your mental health. It takes a huge amount of patience to unravel what is happening for a small baby, especially given postnatal support is so sparse (and also conflicting at the same time). Perhaps you have no tongue tie assessor in travelling distance of where you live. Maybe you do not have the finances for visiting an osteopath to search for birth tension. And, more importantly, maybe it would be easier to just settle for shorter naps than send yourself down the rabbit hole of working out what is going on. Some parents will have a gut feel for which of these factors are affecting their baby, but not everyone will know. Acceptance is sometimes a calmer and more comforting place to be. If your baby's naps are short and you have attempted to rectify this by some of the above but don't seem to be making progress, decide whether it might be easier to sit back and just ride it out. While there might always be a reason for broken sleep, it does not mean that the reason is always easy to find. Or sometimes you can find it, but not do anything about it. It is in these situations that I would urge you to prioritise yourself.

Helping Your Baby to Link Cycles

As well as the acceptance of baby just doing shorter naps, you can try linking the naps together yourself. While baby is not doing it, there is no reason why you cannot do this for them. If your baby is waking after 30–45 minutes and you can see that they need more sleep, or you feel as though you need a bit longer, then resettling them back to sleep is a really good option. When your baby starts to stir as they reach the end of the first sleep cycle when they normally wake, go over to your baby and try:

✧ Holding them and contact napping to lengthen the nap

✧ Feeding them back to sleep

✧ Patting them in their sleep space to see if they might go back off

✧ Picking them up for a cuddle and wind, putting them down once they are drifting off

✧ Popping baby into the sling or pram and going for a walk

There is nothing wrong with helping your baby to elongate their naps. At such a young age, with so many variables affecting their sleep, we do not need to worry about helping babies. As they grow, their tummies mature, and their latches improve, naps should become easier. Until then, get them to sleep however possible! There is no need to worry about any bad habits forming or setting yourself up to fail in the future. Such a thing does not exist, and your baby will lengthen their naps when they feel comfortable and ready to.

Summary

✧ Short day time naps can be common for small babies, but for others they can be a sign that something else is bothering them.

✧ Start with the basics: awake windows and feeding to ensure that baby has the best chance of doing some nice, longer naps.

✧ With newborn babies, you can help them link their cycles by offering a mini feed, cuddling them or finishing the nap off on you. Although don't be a slave to longer naps and embrace the short naps if this is more your style.

✧ Often short naps can be linked to underlying tummy or airway challenges such as tongue ties and food sensitivities. Explore the relevant chapters for lots more information on this.

✧ A baby who can't be put down at all usually means something else is bothering them. So while this is often normalised, there is so much you can do to look into it.

14

Night Waking – What Is and Isn't Possible

Newborn babies wake frequently in the night time, so we shall start this chapter by managing expectations. Your baby is very unlikely to be sleeping through the night in the first 3–4 months of their life and so this is not going to be the aim of this chapter. Small babies need to feed during the night time and long gone are the days of routines and approaches that suggest a baby is left for up to 12 hours at night time at 6 weeks of age. Believe it or not, that approach was a thing. That said, in my time working with so many babies overnight, I had a handful of babies who did sleep through the night for 10–12 hours, from the age of 6 weeks. There was no magic ingredient to these babies. They had a routine, they were well fed and comfortable. At no point were they left to cry or forced to give up night feeds. It always amazed me but I can't claim that it was anything I did other than set them up to be comfortable and content in their nap and bedtimes. Our average newborn will not be doing a full night until they are closer to 6 months, and even then there is huge variety in what a baby is capable of.

While we are not expecting too much from your new baby in the early weeks and months, there is a fine line between not expecting much, versus waking and being unsettled through the entire night. The broken sleep of a newborn has been normalised so much in recent years, that parents who are waking up to every hour assume that this is standard newborn behaviour.

I would imagine that for most of you reading this book, there is some level of improvement that we can make to your baby's night time stretches. Yes, of course babies need to feed in the night time – at no point are we denying them the food that they need. Their tummies are small and so regular feeds are to be expected, but not to the extent that you as a parent are struggling and not getting any sleep. Much like with day time naps, it should be possible for your baby to be put down and to do some stretches of up to a few hours or more during the night time. If your baby is waking every 1–2 hours or more, then know even by just being here, you are on your way to being able to improve that.

To Wake or Not to Wake?

The very first question you will have when it comes to your newborn's night time sleep is whether or not you should wake your newborn baby. You will hear varying views on this and I have certainly heard some weird and wonderful answers to this question in my time. The general rule of thumb that I have always worked by is answered by your baby's weight. When they are first born, babies can lose up to 10 per cent or more of their body weight. They are also very sleepy. For this reason, it is a good idea to wake your baby to feed every 3–4 hours during the night time, more if you are advised to do so by a medical professional if there are weight concerns. If your baby has jaundice, or any health concerns, then you will likely be asked to continue to wake them to feed until these things are sorted.

Once your baby is back up to birth weight, and assuming that they are medically healthy, you can stop waking your baby at night time and let them go for as long as they will sleep for. This is in the night time only. In the day you should continue to wake them every three or so hours, to ensure that they are getting plenty of milk and to stimulate supply if you are breastfeeding. At the point where you stop waking them in the night (often around the two week mark for most), you may get a few longer stretches of sleep every couple of nights. The likelihood though is that they are still little and will probably wake up after 3–5 hours to feed, before then going back off to sleep. If your baby sleeps for longer than this then don't worry. In fact, you may be more uncomfortable than baby if you are still breastfeeding, so may end up waking baby instead! (It is not unusual for babies to start doing some longer stretches of 7–8 hours at around the 8–10 week mark, although this doesn't necessarily last, especially due to the vaccinations which can disrupt sleep for your baby.)

If your baby is fully comfortable and feeding well in the day time, their night time feeds will start to push out and get later as they grow. By following my approach to sleep, I would expect your baby to be well on their way to one night feed in 12 hours at the 4-month mark. This is a process which cannot be forced, but the content of this book is designed for exactly that – promoting brilliant sleep and positive sleep habits for years to come.

Heidi's Journey

I have been lucky that none of my babies have ever given me long and broken nights, aside from in the days following their vaccinations or if they have had a reflux flare-ups. Much of this has been because of my experience of dealing with babies at night time and knowing a handful of things that you will explore in this chapter in order to help them feed, settle and sleep for longer stretches of time. My first slept through the night at 4 months of age and my second baby at 6 months, with my third yet to be decided (she is 3 months as I write this now). At no point did I leave them to cry or have to do any sleep training with them, but used all of the information in this book and they slowly did it themselves!

Lengthening Nights

There is a common misconception that the only way to reduce night time wakes and help a baby sleep better is to leave them to cry. This could not be further from the truth and one of the main messages I have for new parents is exactly this. You do not have to embark on any sleep coaching when your baby is older. Sleep is not about leaving a baby to cry or not. You can successfully set up sleep from early on, so that you avoid needing to do any sleep coaching further down the line. Obviously setbacks do happen, and sleep can sometimes be turned upside-down, which can throw things off course, but otherwise you do not need to feel pushed into either the 'cry' or 'no cry' camp of parenting. By following the advice in this book, you are setting your baby up to have all of the skills and know-how they need to become a brilliant night time sleeper.

Without leaving them to cry then, what exactly can we do to get our babies sleeping for longer at night time? Remember that we are talking about small babies from newborn to 3 or 4 months here, so this is not about forcing them to drop night feeds before they are ready. Rather, it is about a number of tips and tricks that you can have up your sleeve, to start using at night time.

The Mid-Feed Nappy Change

This one seems so simple yet it is often not used by parents. Understandably, when your baby wakes in the night time, you are exhausted. Often half asleep, you pick baby up and feed them. Trying not to fall asleep, you doze or struggle to stay awake while they drink, then put them straight back down so that you can roll over and go back to sleep yourself. Baby then goes back to sleep but wakes again after only an hour or two. The reason? They fell asleep feeding and took only enough to see them back to sleep, rather than a full feed. This happens a lot during the night time and can be improved by a simple nappy change.

You do not need to wake your baby to change their nappy, but in the early months I would highly recommend doing a nappy change when your baby feeds during the night time. As they wake up, offer their feed, but then, if bottle-feeding, stop as they start to slow down. If breastfeeding, you can do this between breasts. By changing your baby's nappy, not only are you laying them flat to help any wind settle and subsequently come back up, but you are also waking them up much like the method of active breastfeeding discussed earlier in the book. By waking them up, you give them a chance to then go back on to the breast or bottle and take more milk. This means they end up having a more wakeful, bigger feed, with the idea that they then sleep for a little bit longer. It is such a simple tip, but one that makes a huge difference to so many babies.

'La Pause'

This technique is French for 'waiting a moment' or 'pausing' before going to your baby. Of course it would only be natural to assume that if your baby makes a noise, they are awake. As your baby starts to stir, you go to them and pick them up, assuming that they need feeding or comfort. What we are not often told is that babies make plenty of noise in their sleep. They may even appear to open their eyes, move their limbs and, generally, their lighter sleep looks a lot more wakeful than ours does as adults. For this reason, as a new parent you would expect that your baby needs you, but the opposite is often the case.

If your baby is making noise or grunting and moving around, leave them be. If your baby starts to cry, this is at the point where you will go to them and see what they need, most likely a feed, or perhaps a nappy change or burp. That said, before you go to them, you may want to try 'la pause'. This is a simple pause from the point of your baby starting to cry, to see if they resettle or not. There is no set length to this pause, but you may want to give your baby a minute or two, and if they are still upset then go straight to them.

This pause and break before going to them is not letting your baby cry it out, but really simply just giving them a moment to see if they will resettle by themselves. From experience of sleeping in a room with babies for years, I have heard babies do all sorts in their sleep and crying out is one of them. Sometimes a baby is not even awake when they are crying, so by giving it a minute or two, you may end up with a baby who goes back to sleep without you needing to intervene. Anecdotally, French babies seem to sleep through the night earlier than in the UK, and certainly many of my French clients have had the babies who sleep through earlier on (from 6 weeks), so it could potentially be one of the factors involved.

Bring up the Wind

As with a nappy change, the majority of parents will aim to feed and get baby back down to sleep as quickly as possible to avoid any prolonged periods of being awake. Becoming a new parent with multiple night wakes is exhausting, so it makes sense to minimise your time awake and protect your sleep. I am going to argue in favour of spending more time awake though… When you spend extra time winding your baby during a night feed, there is much more likelihood of a longer stretch of sleep afterwards. So many babies fall asleep on the breast or bottle having taken in wind while they are feeding. This wind then sits in their stomach and will decide to come up at an inconvenient moment, probably an hour or two after going into their sleep space.

When this wind comes up, they wake and cry out. Their parent then assumes they need feeding again, and so the cycle continues. Baby feeds for a bit, takes in wind, they then do not bring the wind up and fall back to sleep. Such a huge percentage of my clients make significant changes to their baby's sleep by implementing proper winding during a night feed. This could be halfway through the feed, after the nappy change, or at the end of a night feed. Do not be scared to wake baby up as they will be naturally sleepy afterwards anyway, so a little bit of winding is not going to cause too much disruption. If they are not bringing up any wind, try laying them flat on the bed next to you for a minute and then picking them up again. You can also try some tummy rubbing. Most babies are quite sleepy during the night so wind may not come up as easily as in the day time, but do at least try for 10 minutes before putting baby down. If anything, the upright position will help baby settle their milk before they go back to sleep.

Try Resettling First

As you will have picked up on, I am all about getting your baby totally comfortable and night times are no exception. A baby with a full, but not too full, tummy will sleep easily and happily if they have no underlying tummy or airway concerns. However, a baby with a very full tummy, or a digestive system that is overloaded by feeding too frequently, will sleep for shorter chunks of time. For this reason, if your newborn baby wakes up after only an hour or two since last feeding, try winding them with a nice cuddle over your shoulder before immediately assuming they need food again.

It is only natural to want to feed your baby up, and assume that they only wake in the night for food. The reality is though, they may be waking with a burp, wind, tummy ache or any other number of reasons. A night wake does not always indicate hunger. If the time since your last feed seems quite recent, then try reset-tling baby without feeding just to start with. This is not to say you are going to hold back a feed from your baby. If your baby needs food, then they need food! Yet by trying to settle them back to sleep, if it is something like a burp that needs to come up, they will then go back down for another chunk of time before feeding again. The benefit of this is that they do not feed too frequently which then in turn makes them more comfortable. The knock-on effect of being more comfortable is, of course, better sleep.

Assuming a baby is gaining weight and feeding is becoming well established with a good transfer of milk during each feed, then it is unlikely they will need feeding again within the hour. By naturally trying out some of these techniques, night sleep is going to start to lengthen before you have even considered any other sleep strategies or approaches.

Working Together

Multiple night wakings in the early months can be exhausting and while sharing the wake-ups is not always possible for some single-parent families, those with two resident parents may choose to conquer the night wake-ups together. This will depend on a number of factors including method of feeding (breast versus bottle) and lifestyle (work commitments having a big emphasis). If breastfeeding, it is natural to assume that the nights all fall to the breastfeeding parent, however the reality is that both parents can be involved, particularly with a baby who wakes up frequently. If baby wakes and it is not quite yet time for a feed as above, trying to resettle baby without a feed may potentially be easier for the non-milk-producing partner. This is because babies often tend to smell the milk and this may mean that they settle back less easily without the feed, whereas the other parent may have more success at settling baby. Producing milk is not the only factor though, and it will of course depend on whether or not the other non-feeding partner has confidence in handling baby and is used to doing so. Should lifestyle factors allow, it is worth having a chat about it should you find yourself in a world of multiple night wakes and starting to become more exhausted.

Case Study: Baby Amy, aged 10 weeks

At 10 weeks of age, Amy was still waking every 1–2 hours in the night for a feed. Amy's parents had seen a lactation consultant who suggested that this was normal newborn behaviour, yet many of their friends' babies were doing longer stretches. When I visited Amy at her home, she was a contented and calm baby who didn't appear to be suffering from any discomfort. As well as implementing a day time routine, we also looked at the possibility of settling Amy back to sleep when she woke without feeding her every single time. Mum and Dad spent a week settling Amy back to sleep if she woke before four hours since her last feed, and she was soon doing a stretch of 6–7 hours. Amy had not been left to cry, but simply settled back to sleep in another way rather than feeding. Amy was able to go much longer between feeds than she was showing, and just needed the chance to be picked up, winded and then put back down again, which aided her doing longer stretches.

Dealing with Broken Nights and Parenting

Over the years, I have spent thousands of nights getting up with small babies and so I am well aware of what it is to be tired – not tired-from-a-night-out tired, but tiredness that consumes you as your birth hormones start to regulate but your baby keeps waking! The first few weeks will go by in a flash, before you even really start to feel tired. Then slowly, but surely, the tiredness will creep up on you. This is so often why looking at your baby's sleep at around that time becomes more needed. Parents are searching for a way to manage both the tiredness that they feel with their busy everyday lives of running a home, family, career, pets and everything and anything else that we juggle on a daily basis.

Being tired and looking after a small baby is no mean feat. In honest conversations, I have often heard parents describe going into work and doing a full day much less tiring then being at home with baby. Maternity leave is not all coffee shops and play dates. A lot of the days are spent simply trying to put one foot in front of the other and wondering if you will ever sleep again. If this is you, and you are feeling exhausted, then please know that this is super-normal. Having a baby who wakes up in the night time is exhausting, no matter how much you love them! Whereas we used to rely on family to help us out in close-knit communities in years gone by, most of us simply do not have that anymore, which leads to burnout and exhaustion, which can result in the 'baby blues'.

As a night nanny, I was very aware of the benefit of a full night's sleep for a client. Some of the clients that I had were not just super-rich with tons of extra cash to spare, but real-life families who recognised the impact that disrupted sleep would have on them for a long period of time. There were also families where mum had an illness that meant sleep was even more important to her. On other occasions, my service had been gifted by a family member as they were too far away to help, but knew that supporting the mother's sleep would be extremely important. If I could gift a full night's sleep to everyone, I certainly would. In the meantime, here are some ways in which families have dealt with lack of sleep when navigating their parenting journeys that might help you:

✧ Offering a bottle for one of baby's night feeds. Often, mum would pump when I arrived at 9pm and then it meant that

I could do the 10/11pm feed when baby woke. This gave the mother a long stretch of sleep before needing to feed again around 2/3am or whenever baby woke. A partner can also do this for you, so that you are getting at least one stretch of unbroken sleep at the beginning of the night. I always felt like a 4–5-hour stretch made me feel significantly brighter the next day, as opposed to only 2–3-hour chunks.

✧ Asking your partner to either share the nights if you are open to bottles alongside breastfeeding, or just to do one night every now and then so that you can catch up on sleep. Do not underestimate the power of one full night's sleep, even if it is just every now and then. It can do wonders for how you feel and your mental health too.

✧ 'Sleep when the baby sleeps' is a seriously outdated phrase as it assumes that your baby sleeps, but also that you have nothing else to do. However, there is power in the nap! Even the smallest 10-minute nap can help reset the body and give you a little more energy. There is always something to do in the house, but try leaning into the idea that this fourth trimester is a very short period of time. The priority is still yourself and your baby, so have that cup of tea, sit down on the sofa and allow your eyes to close before your baby then wakes up again. Feeding side by side and sleeping together for a nap is also a lovely way of releasing oxytocin and relaxing you. The dishwasher can wait.

✧ Tiredness can feel like the end of the world when you start your day feeling exhausted from a very broken night. It can undoubtedly affect your sanity. While tiredness is inevitable, if you can focus on just getting through the next hour, and then the following, this can be really helpful. Taking it step by step, little by little, will help you to not project that the whole day is going to be terrible. By lunchtime, you will probably have a little more spring in your step again and your mood will lift.

✧ Remember to look after yourself. It is so much easier said than done but drinking enough water and eating good foods can make a huge difference. A lot of our grab-and-go food is not as nutritious as it could be. You may not have time to make proper food to begin with, but pull in favours from friends, or make use of healthy ready-made meals alongside good quality supplements to support your body. Without you, your baby wouldn't be here so you have to prioritise yourself.

Summary

✧ Night wakes are common and to be expected in small babies. Until baby is back to birth weight, it is suggested you wake baby regularly to ensure that they are getting the food they need to be able to sleep well.

✧ There are many tools you can use as a parent to help night sleepings lengthen once baby is gaining weight as expected; these include nappy changes, pausing to see if baby can settle back to sleep and also winding baby between feeds to help them go longer.

✧ Sleep is an important part of birth recovery, milk production and generally feeling able to cope with parenting a small baby. Allowing your partner to give a bottle feed, napping with baby and sharing the nights are some of the possible ways of dealing with broken sleep until baby starts to stretch out during the night time.

15

Introducing Self-Settling for Sleep

In addition to the many factors affecting sleep that we have explored in this book so far, there is one more factor that will influence your baby's sleep as they grow and develop and that is *how* they fall to sleep. This is usually referred to as 'self-settling' or 'independent settling' and refers to a baby's ability to be able to fall asleep on their own without needing any help and support. Please be mindful that this is not their ability to 'self-soothe' which refers to them being able to be in control and regulate their own emotions. This is a skill that does not develop until much later into their early adulthood years (studies suggest around age 21).

The concept of a baby falling asleep on their own attracts much controversy in the sleep world, with some sleep scientists suggesting that it is necessary for good-quality sleep for the whole family. Others suggest that falling asleep without an adult is an alien concept that has been invented in the Western world as a by-product of our busy lives and lack of support. Most parents are now in a state of confusion when it comes to their baby's ability to self-settle, especially given the overload of information on social media. In my humble, yet extremely experienced, opinion, the ability of a baby to be able to fall asleep on their own can have a huge impact on how well they sleep during the night time and for their day time naps. When we unlock a baby's ability to settle to sleep on their own, there are often huge improvements in their sleep overall. Nevertheless, it is not the only variable that affects sleep and will often not work if other factors have not been addressed.

During the first three months of your baby's life, the way in which they fall asleep is going to be very dependent on you. Naturally, they will need more support and, as we have explored, there are so many factors affecting their sleep early on that the likelihood is that they will need your assistance. A baby who has reflux will only really sleep upright on you until their symptoms are better. A baby who takes in air while feeding will find it hard to settle themselves to sleep as their tummy feels bloated. We know that all of these things, and more, can vastly impact your baby's sleep early on. This is why there is no need to force or push independent sleep in those early months and it is much better to accept the idea that your baby most likely needs your help to fall to sleep.

Some of the possible ways that you may wish to help your new baby fall asleep in the first few months include:

✧ Rocking to sleep

✧ Feeding your baby to sleep

✧ Walking baby for sling naps

✧ Pushing baby in the pram

✧ Bouncing on the yoga ball while holding them

✧ Using a dummy to settle them

✧ Safely co-sleeping

✧ Patting and side settling to sleep

There is simply not just one way to do sleep with a newborn. You will probably find yourself trying a combination of these things at different times of day, depending on your lifestyle, whether or not you have other children, and how you are finding life with a small baby. While some parents are really happy rocking a baby to sleep, others may not have the time and therefore baby will end up napping on the go. You simply cannot spoil your baby, so do not worry about the way in which they fall asleep. If it is working for you, then it is working. It really is as straightforward as that.

Low Pressure Practice

We have explored the idea of practising putting your baby down for naps in previous chapters, with the understanding being that your baby gets used to being put down for some naps. This very low pressure practice enables your baby to start to recognise a short bedtime routine that happens before they go down for a nap or at night. It also enables them to start getting used to their sleep space. Therefore, I recommend that if you are keen on establishing sleep habits early on, that you practise putting baby down for one nap a day from as early on as you feel ready. At this stage, your baby is likely to be between a few weeks to a few months old so you will probably get them to sleep before putting them down. This works perfectly and the very first step that comes before self-settling is having a baby who is happy to be put down. Do not forget that if you cannot get your baby down at all, there is likely to be a reason.

Sleep-Shaping Techniques

Once you have mastered the art of being able to put your baby down for naps or into their crib in the evening, the next step is to start to move towards them being able to fall asleep with a little less support. This is not a mandatory rite of passage for babies and plenty of parents will continue to help their babies to sleep well into the toddler years – and there is nothing wrong with this. If sleep is working for you, then there is no reason to try and change it. That said, my assumption would be that if you are reading a self-settling chapter in a baby book, then you would like to move towards helping your baby to learn to fall asleep on their own. If this is the case, you are in the very best hands and this is something we can work on so gently that your baby will hardly be aware that they are doing it on their own... until they are! This is not about leaving your baby to cry, or even sleep training, but just about using a consistent approach to settling them to sleep which allows them to unlock their true sleep potential.

Many of my clients ask me whether it is actually possible that a small baby can fall asleep without any help. We are sold the idea that it is biologically normal for a baby to need help to get to sleep, which I would agree with – babies need lots of help. My problem with the way in which this is portrayed is that parents are not also told that lots of babies can also fall asleep without support, even from a young age. I have watched many a baby of just a few days to a few weeks old (including my own at times), be put down into their sleep space and look around then gradually fall asleep on their own. The ability to fall asleep is something that we are all programmed to do from day one – it exists for every baby. At the beginning, some babies find this easier than others, and this usually comes down to what else they have going on both in terms of their tummies, tension and temperament. You will be surprised at the number of clients I have had who have been shocked at how easily their baby has settled to sleep, just by giving them the confidence to practise. It really does not have to be about either leaving them to cry or always holding them. There is a wonderful in-between that exists where you can both hold and cuddle your baby for naps, and then slowly start to unravel their ability to settle themselves to sleep.

When Is the Right Time?

The decision to start practising independent settling to sleep is one that is so family specific that it would be impossible for me to give you a time at which this needs to happen. Each and every baby is born into such different settings and surroundings. You may have other children and have had to practise putting your baby down from day one, or this may be your first baby and you have no intention of working on settling for months to come. In my approach to shaping sleep, I like to start practising self-settling any time from 6 weeks of age, but by around 10–12 weeks of age is when I feel that it starts to have the most impact.

The way in which a baby settles to sleep has little impact on their sleep in the first three months of their life, but as they start to creep towards four months of age their settling can start to impact the length of naps and potentially night wakings too. If possible, I would support every parent with a programme of gentle sleep-shaping in months three or four, so that by four months the baby would be happy drifting off in their safe sleep space.

This is not to say that this will always be what they do, or that you cannot do it other ways too. You can absolutely mix it up and some of my fondest memories are of 4pm TV naps where my babies slept on me. At the same time though, I could pop them down for naps during the day time so that I could take out my laptop and do some work. It is ok, and possible, to have both a baby who falls asleep on their own and that also still has cuddle and contact naps. The best of both worlds, in my opinion.

Before you start working on unlocking your baby's potential to fall to sleep by themselves, I would like you to consider the following:

✧ Is feeding well established with baby taking full feeds and with no concerns about weight gain?

✧ Is baby comfortable? Settling to sleep unaided is only going to happen with a baby who is able to drift off without any wind or tummy ache and so on. If you are still on your journey to a comfortable baby, possibly now is not the right time to get started.

✧ Do you truly believe? By this, I mean the ability of a baby to fall asleep on their own. I have full confidence that your baby is able to do this, but this does not mean that you do too. You have to want and believe this to be possible – if you have doubts about the approach you are taking, it is not going to work.

✧ Can you practise for at least one nap a day and/or the evening sleep for at least a week? If you are travelling or have busy days coming up full of commitments, then it is unlikely to be the right time for you.

Sleep-Shaping Approaches

While many approaches will talk about putting your baby down 'drowsy but awake', for this approach you will require your baby to be awake. Not drowsy, or asleep, but awake. The reason I choose not to use the drowsy but awake option is simply that drowsy is subjective and to one parent that will be a baby who is fully asleep, and to another a baby who is hardly sleepy at all. It just adds confusion and means clients get stuck in a halfway house of trying to put their baby down at the right time. The reality is, you need your baby to be awake, but calm. This means that they haven't just gone straight from their play gym to their cot within minutes (being therefore overstimulated). Instead, they have had some wind-down time with you, are fed, winded, comfortable and ready to sleep, but not yet asleep.

The second factor to consider when starting to work on self-settling, is your baby's awake window. They are much more likely to settle easily if you are mindful of their awake window. For example, if you are practising self-settling with a 12-week-old, their awake window is around 1 hour and up to 1 hour 30 minutes. This means that I would probably start the process of putting them down slightly before this point. Awake windows are very much guidelines, so start with the suggested time for your baby's age and then add on or take away 10–15 minutes each side, depending on how your baby responds.

Once your baby is at the end of their awake window and is ready to sleep, and is calm but awake, then you can start the process of trying to settle them down to sleep. In previous chapters we already introduced the idea of a naptime or bedtime routine, which you may already be doing. This will involve going into the room that your baby will be sleeping in and implementing their little routine which probably looks something like:

✦ Feed or top-up feed if baby needs it

✦ Wind baby well

✦ A nappy change

✧ Into a swaddle or sleeping bag of choice

✧ Read a story

✧ Sing a song and have a cuddle

Once you reach the stage of cuddling baby on your shoulder, they will hopefully be very ready to sleep. At this point, you can then lower them down into their sleep space, by lowering their legs and feet to touch the mattress first, followed by their body and then their head. As your baby is put down, you can use your voice to make calming 'shh'ing' noises. Often, a baby will prefer to be put down on to their side, then patted and 'shh'd' for a minute or so, before then being rolled straight on to their back. This can help reduce the likelihood of their arms startling them which can cause them to get upset.

Once your baby is in their cot, you then have two differing approaches for helping them learn to settle themselves to sleep. Neither of these involve leaving your baby to cry as this is not necessary or something I would recommend with a baby at this age. We can simply start to shape your baby's sleep in the most responsive way, just by practising the art of being put to sleep.

The Baby Steps Approach

Depending on how you usually get your baby to sleep now will depend on where you start when it comes to baby steps. The baby steps approach is about slowly moving from one way of settling baby, to using a different way until you slowly unravel each layer, ending up with a baby who is falling asleep on their own.

A perfect example of this is clients who wish to move away from feeding their baby to sleep. Feeding your baby to sleep is not an issue, unless you do not want to be doing it. If you wish to move away from it, then your first stage of baby steps would be to practise settling your baby by rocking them to sleep in your arms, instead of feeding. This gentle transition means that they are still fully supported to sleep, but are not on the breast as they fall asleep. The same would work for bottle-feeding too. Once your baby is happily being rocked to sleep, then you can either stick with this for longer, or move to the next stage.

The stages of baby steps can be defined by you, but as a rough guideline they look something like:

1. Rocking your baby to sleep or holding and cuddling them to sleep (if you have been previously feeding baby).

2. Putting baby down into their sleep space and patting, 'shh'ing' and staying with them to fall to sleep.

3. Putting baby into their sleep space and holding your hand on them, without too much movement, e.g. taking away the patting.

4. Putting your baby down, and then sitting close by to reassure them with 'shh'ing', but not touching them.

Once you have reached the point where your baby is able to fall asleep with you close by, you have a baby who is falling asleep by themselves. These stages can be done slowly, over a number of weeks or months, or you can speed them up and move between them every 3–5 days or so, if you wish. There is no set programme to remember, this is not about troubleshooting or fixing sleep. This is purely about having a consistent way of settling your baby so that they slowly learn to be put down into their sleep space. Not only that, but they also become confident, very gently, that they can drift off in their safe sleep space, by themselves.

The Cuddle and Calm Approach

When we cuddle and calm our babies, they feel safe and secure. Cuddling your baby helps release oxytocin, which can also help them feel more relaxed and fall into sleep. The cuddle and calm approach is very straightforward. It is a way of practising putting your baby down just to see if they can drift off to sleep on their own. Again, this is not about leaving them to cry and you will respond to any crying with cuddles and calmness, just as the name suggests.

Once you have carried your baby's little mini nap routine (or bedtime routine, if using this in the evening), you will then put baby down into their sleep space, saying goodnight and stepping to the side. As I have mentioned before, sometimes it really is just about practice for a baby. They will so often surprise you. Watch your baby and see what they then do. If they are full, winded and ready for sleep, they may look around, make some noises and drift off to sleep. This is the best-case scenario, and is entirely possible. However, we also know that they are lots of different variables that affect a baby's sleep, so this will not always be the case.

Babies do make noise both in their sleep and when they are settling to sleep. I encourage you to give your baby the space they need, and only step in if they start to cry. Moaning and chatting away can be a process of starting to settle off to sleep, so just don't jump in too quickly! If your baby does start to cry, go to them straight away and pick them up. You can soothe them on your shoulder, pat and rub their back to check for any wind, and then snuggle them until they are nice and calm again. So often, this is when a few stuck burps will come up and you will realise that they had wind. Once baby is calm and ready to try again, lower them back down into their cot again and wait close by. By practising putting our baby down into their sleep space, we are showing them that they are in a safe space and they can build up their confidence to knowing that this is where sleep happens. It will not necessarily happen on the first attempt and can take a little bit of time, but slowly you should be able to move towards them being able to be put down, with little support.

With both of the practice sleep approaches, as your baby is still so little, you only need to commit to this for a short period of time. You might decide to try for up to 15 minutes and I would advise a maximum of 30 minutes at most for a newborn. The younger your baby, the less time you need to try for as then you run into them becoming very overtired and missing the window in which they will settle easily. During this trying time, tune into your baby's communication as this is also key in working out what is going on for them. If their cry stops easily when you pick them up and they sound tired, then you are likely to see some success. However, if your baby cries as soon as they are put on to their back and they are not soothed when picked up, or sound very distressed, then I would recommend that you tune into this and your gut feeling. While we have explored other reasons for not sleeping in huge detail within this book, it may still be that there is a reason that they are not taking to being put down. In this scenario, I would encourage you to read back through the chapters on air intake, reflux and oral tension, to try and help baby become more comfortable before revisiting this chapter.

A few weeks can make a huge difference in the life cycle of a newborn baby, so try not to be put off if you give this a go at say 10 weeks, when you think your baby is doing well and seems settled, but then they don't take to it. A few weeks later, their gut may be stronger, their latch may be easier, and their tension less of an issue, so they may take to it much more easily. I cannot stress enough that your baby has to be fully comfortable to be able to settle on their own. It is not a question of whether they have the ability to do it or not, they absolutely do and they were practising it in utero.

Heidi's Journey

One of the best skills I ever taught my children was to learn to fall asleep on their own. When I watch them now, at varying ages, I truly think it is the most magical thing. They chat, they sing, they look around, and they drift off in a space that they know and believe is safe and snug to them. I have never had to fight them to go to bed and on the odd occasion they have even asked to go. I love that they love sleep. This is all down to the way in which we were able to shape their sleep from early on. Without having to troubleshoot their sleep later down the line, we were able to put into place the ingredients needed for confident self-settling from early on. This of course only came when they were fully comfortable and reflux free, but it worked. For me, this was important and leaves me in a position now where I can choose to cuddle them to sleep or stay with them if I want to, or feel they need it, but they can also do it totally on their own too. It is the best gift I have given them.

They just need the right conditions in the outside world too, with their physiological comfort levels being at the very centre of their ability to sleep without too much support.

The Four-Month Sleep Regression

The word 'regression' can fill any parent with dread, especially when it comes to sleep. Let's say your baby is already waking up a few times a night as it stands, the concept of a regression and sleep getting worse can be really anxiety-inducing. This is why the phrase regression really should be renamed to 'progression' because your baby is constantly developing and moving forwards, not backwards. The four-month sleep progression is the only sleep regression that is actually based on science and it happens usually at around the four-month mark, but sometimes a little earlier and sometimes a little later.

During this period, your baby will start to have more defined sleep cycles and become more aware of transitioning through their sleep cycles too. This means that as they come towards the end of that 30–45-minute cycle, they may well stir more readily and easily than they had done in the months running up to this time. During the four-month sleep progression period, your baby may potentially have shorter naps, more night wakes and be harder to settle to sleep. I want to reassure you that this is so often only temporary, and for lots of babies it comes and goes without sleep looking any different at all.

One of the many reasons I am so passionate about this book is because by making your baby comfortable and confident at sleeping, the four-month change to sleep means that you are unlikely to see the regression cause too much of an issue for your baby's sleep. When a baby is settled, has practised being put down to sleep and is on the way to learning to settle themselves to sleep, the four-month sleep progression becomes much less of an issue to sleep. For many of my clients, their baby's sleep stays exactly the same. Please do not spend your time worrying about this happening. Even if your baby does start waking up more or having shorter naps, you have all you need in this book to be able to get back on track again. If sleep starts to slip, then check in on all of the points that you have learned already to be able to get it back, including:

✧ Has feeding changed? Is baby still full from feeds? At four months, they often start becoming distracted, looking around and being fussier during day time feeds. This can affect night time feeds. For this reason, doing day time feeds in a calm and quiet place can be really helpful.

✧ Has your baby recently been introduced to formula? This is often a time that parents start to add in bottles to a baby's diet and the change of milk can cause the tummy to become upset – therefore the root cause of the sleep regression actually may be their comfort levels rather than the regression itself.

✧ Did your baby recently have vaccinations? Vaccines can cause temporary sleep disturbances, and also an increase in, or the start of, reflux symptoms. Work on their gut health if this appears to be a correlation and give sleep a few weeks to self-correct.

If your baby's sleep becomes very challenging during this four-month time and you have accounted for their comfort levels, alongside all of the above variables, then it may be that helping unlock their self-settling ability will help sleep fall back into place. There is no need to wait until a regression is over to work on sleep and, if anything, this age is a great time to start to implement some of the sleep strategies we have covered in this chapter.

Summary

✦ There is a lot of controversy around a baby learning to settle to sleep on their own but there really does not need to be. Shaping your baby's sleep from the beginning is entirely possible and this removes the need for sleep training or 'crying it out' further down the line.

✦ Practice makes... sleep! By putting baby down every now and then, you are giving them the chance to fall asleep on their own. Many babies can do it, but just don't get the chance to.

✦ Baby needs to be full, comfortable and not too over- or undertired for settling to happen easily. Take these variables into account and tackle them before attempting to work on baby learning to settle.

✦ Choose a settling approach that fits you and your baby best. None of these approaches include leaving your baby to cry; they are super-gentle and responsive.

✦ As time goes by, and with more practice, your baby will slowly learn to settle themselves to sleep, giving you the option to put them down as well as cuddle them if you would prefer.

✦ There is no right or wrong approach when it comes to your baby's sleep and you should absolutely do whatever it is that feels best for you.

16

Combination Feeding

While we have focused mostly on sleep and your baby's comfort levels, I wanted to include some information on one of the topics that I feel is hugely underrated in the postnatal period – combination feeding (which we discussed briefly in the Chapter 5). Combination feeding is the ability to give your baby both breast and bottles so that they become used to feeding via both methods. This means that other people can feed your baby and gives you the option as to whether to feed your baby exclusively breastmilk or to balance that out with one or more formula feeds in a 24-hour period.

Combination feeding is rarely talked about as a feeding option on its own. Most parents will stumble across it when they find themselves in a position to give up breastfeeding for various reasons, rather than actively choosing it to start with. It is one of my strong beliefs that more babies would get breastmilk for longer if parents knew that combination feeding was a possibility, rather than assuming the choice always has to be between breast or formula.

There are many benefits to combination feeding and these can include:

✧ Bottle feeds allow another parent or family member/friend to be able to feed your baby. This works to help spread the load but also if the mother is due back to work early on.

✧ Baby does not develop a preference for breast only, which gives more flexibility in the future with the option to switch to bottles entirely or to add bottles to baby's diet.

✧ Baby gets used to the taste of formula which means that it can be added in with ease without worrying about them refusing it.

✧ Baby continues to have breastmilk for longer, being supported by formula too, rather than mum giving up breastfeeding entirely. This means baby continues to receive the antibodies and goodness of breastmilk too.

✧ Mum has the option to have a break from feeding, enabling her to go out for a day, or even a night away should she wish.

✧ Breastfeeding is wonderful but can, for some, be one of the factors affecting maternal mental health. By taking off the pressure, breastfeeding could be more likely to last for longer and make mum more able to cope with the option of doing both.

If breastfeeding comes easily and naturally to you and your baby, then it can be the best choice of feeding for both mother and baby. However, the postnatal support that most women receive for breastfeeding is thin on the ground, not to mention the lack of support for babies with sensitive gut issues and tongue ties. These things combined mean that, for a lot of women, breastfeeding can be really full-on. If this sounds like you, I want to reassure you that there is a way in which you can continue to feed your baby just as you wanted to, but with an option to help both of your journeys along by being able to give baby the breast and formula too. It does not have to be all or nothing, whether we are talking about feeding, contact napping or any area of parenting. These huge choices we feel we have to make are actually polarised to the extreme. Many of my clients find that combination feeding is a great middle ground option and feel relieved knowing that they can, in fact, do both.

Introducing a Bottle

In order to be able to combination feed, you do of course need your baby to be able to take a bottle. General guidance is often to introduce a bottle at six weeks of age, but I find that this is too late for lots of babies. Ideally, baby will be happily breastfeeding before a bottle is introduced as this means that they are less likely to go on breast strike (refusing the breast in favour of the bottle). However, if breastfeeding is taking a long time to settle down then you may find yourself introducing a bottle sooner. In my opinion, anything from two weeks onwards is fine to introduce a bottle regularly as part of your baby's feeding plan, with some babies of course needing bottles earlier than this, for example if they have jaundice or are struggling with weight gain.

Before introducing the bottle we need to ensure that your latch during breastfeeding is going well and there are no challenges or problems, such as a shallow latch or baby pulling on and off. If, for whatever reason, your baby is struggling with breastfeeding, then you will need to work on this before introducing the bottle. It is always worth seeking the support of a lactation consultant in those early days to help with attachment and positioning. If breastfeeding feels painful, then look into tongue ties and see a practitioner with the correct qualifications to assess and treat a tie. Tongue ties can affect not only breastfeeding but bottle-feeding too. A lot of the babies that refuse the bottle early on are those with undiagnosed oral tension and ties.

Once breastfeeding is well established, you can then choose a regular time of day to give your baby a bottle. This might be a mid-morning feed, or more popular is the evening bottle which partners can get involved in. It is a good idea to choose a bottle feed at the same time each day as this helps with baby's acceptance of the bottle and also with your milk supply settling into a routine too. Depending on when you are introducing the bottle, you may wish to continue to give expressed breastmilk in the bottle to start with, rather than formula straight away. We know that supply is easily affected by dropping feeds in the early weeks, so if you are introducing a bottle in the first six weeks or so, know that if you totally drop that feed rather than pump to replace the feed, there is a chance that your supply could reduce. Lots of parents are ok with this, as they know that they will be using formula. Yet, if you have any doubt as to whether you might want to go back to feeding baby exclusively again, I recommend starting with a bottle of breastmilk and then transitioning from there.

Breastfeeding works on a demand and supply basis, so if you are giving baby a bottle but want to maintain your milk supply, then you will need to pump at roughly the same time as feeding your baby. Portable breast pumps now make this a lot easier as you could pump as you are feeding baby the bottle. You can also ask a partner to feed baby the bottle while you pump. Or you could pump just before, or just after, the bottle. Only pump the amount of milk that you need for your baby's feed. If you find that pumping in one session does not produce enough milk for one bottle, then you can also try pumping the second side at the first feed in the morning, or catching your let-down throughout the day by using a milk collector (a small silicone pot that attaches to the alternate nipple while feeding from the other side) to top up what you have managed to get in your pumping session.

If all of this pumping sounds like a complete faff (which it can be – let's be honest), especially if you have other children or busy life commitments, then you can also opt to introduce formula straight away. When you first introduce this, I recommend starting with a morning feed so that you have the whole day to see if baby reacts to the formula milk at all, rather than in an evening just before they go to bed. There are many different types of formula available and you can read more on your baby's tummy and formula milks in Chapter 10.

Heidi's Journey

As a busy working Mummy, being able to give my babies a bottle has been an essential part of our feeding journey. I knew from experience that nipple confusion was not really a concern as long as I did things properly. Although my third baby struggled more with the bottle until her tongue tension was improved, they have all taken the bottle and we were able to interchange between breast and bottle so easily. On busy days, they might have more breast and on work days, they might have more bottles, depending on if I was around to help or not. It worked for us and I believe also made my breastfeeding journey last longer, as I was able to have flexibility.

Bottle Refusal

How easily your baby takes a bottle will depend on a number of factors including when you introduce the bottle itself. We have explored the idea of introducing a bottle early on but this will not be the case for everyone. Each feeding journey brings about its own unique challenges, and planning to give a bottle and then actually giving a bottle are two different concepts. It is so easy for time just to fly on by with a newborn and, before you know it, baby is now a few months old and refusing to take it. This is such a common challenge for many parents, but it can be overcome. Don't give up on your desire to combination feed if that is what you would like to do. I have learned so many ways of helping babies to take the bottle in my time. One of the very first jobs I used to visit parents for would be to get baby to take the bottle. It can take a while but it is entirely possible in the early months.

First off, if you have a baby that is refusing to take a bottle then do have them checked for tongue tie and oral tension. While they may be able to breastfeed well, these babies will so often refuse any kind of bottle or dummy. The teats can trigger their sensitive gag reflex, related to the tongue tie, and they will generally refuse to drink it. They may also struggle to control the flow and suction on to the nipple due to low tongue function, which means they find bottle-feeding quite stressful. So many of the babies that I have worked with who show bottle refusal end up having tongue ties or oral tensions. It is easy to dismiss this if they are feeding well other-wise, but it would always be a starting point for me.

Assuming your baby has no oral ties and tension, but is still point-blank refusing the bottle, then you can start to work your way through the following list of things to try. Remember that, as with most other things in the fourth trimester including sleep, feeding, and getting to the root cause of any discomfort, this will be a process. It won't necessarily happen on day one. It can take time, and this is where many parents often give up, assuming that it will never happen. Perseverance and consistency are two terms that you will get used to in parenting, and they start now!

1. Offer the bottle to your baby by touching and teasing their top lip. This allows for the same open mouth movement that baby would do to latch on to the breast. Try not to just force the bottle nipple into baby's mouth. You ideally want them to open wide for it and take it in by themselves.

2. Try offering the bottle at different times during a feed. You can try when baby is really hungry, in the middle of a breastfeed (by taking baby off and then trying the bottle), and also towards the end of a feed too. Some babies will take the bottle if very hungry, and others will be more open to it if they have just had a little bit of breast milk first.

3. Never force the bottle on baby and stop if they are crying. Negative associations with the bottle and feeding aversions can happen to babies who are forced to take something that they otherwise would prefer not to. Use a positive and upbeat tone when talking to baby around the bottle.

4. Sing to your baby and move around the room when offering the bottle. Some babies will drink much more readily if there is movement, like a gentle sway/rock or walking as this can act as a calming tool.

5. The left side lying position can be a really effective position for baby to take the bottle in. This is when your baby is lying on their left side, with their head higher than their body. This mimics breastfeeding positions, and can make a baby feel more secure.

6. Mix up the positions that you offer the bottle in, and try not to always use the classic cradle hold. Many babies prefer facing their parent, so for example on your knees propped up, or on a cushion so that they can look at you for reassurance when feeding.

7. Try one or two different bottle teats, but there is no point in buying every single bottle brand. If a baby will not take a bottle, then there is likely a reason why (often tongue tie or reflux), rather than it being the bottle itself. You should try a couple of differing teat shapes – something that best mimics your breast and nipple shape. Some have smaller flatter nipples, and others are longer and wider. There is not one perfect bottle brand for each and every baby.

8. In a scenario where baby is really refusing, sometimes having the TV on can be a distraction. While I wouldn't recommend the television for babies of this age ordinarily, for a very short-term fix of getting them to take the bottle, it can work well.

Continue to offer your baby the bottle once a day (twice if you are really needing baby to take the bottle) and offer for up to 15–30 minutes. If by this point they haven't taken it, then feed them as you usually would. On average, it can take a few weeks of trying these things and consistent practice to get baby to become open to taking it. You should then be able to interchange between bottles and breastfeeding more easily, assuming that breastfeeding latch and milk transfer is going well. Remember that if baby finds breast-feeding difficult for any of the reasons we have explored, then there is still a chance they can prefer the bottle. This is why having their latch assessed and seeing an osteo alongside a tongue tie practi-tioner, gives you the very best chance of breastfeeding AND bottle-feeding going well for you.

A Combi-Feeding Routine

Each and every baby is different in their feeding style and requirements, however if you have successfully managed to get your baby to take a bottle, then you can start to work out which feeds you will do as bottles versus breastfeeds. I tend to recommend working this out based on criteria including whether or not you want anyone else to help with feeds, whether the bottle may help the nap or sleep following the bottle (e.g. evening), and how easily you can space the bottles so that your supply adjusts if you are going to introduce formula. In a typical day time routine, you will likely have feeds every three hours or so. If just giving one bottle a day, I would recommend the evening feed as this is when your supply is naturally lower anyway. If more than one, I would space the bottles throughout the day time, remembering that if you end up doing more bottles than breast, there is still a small chance that baby will refuse the breast at some point.

An example day time combi-feeding routine might look like:

7am	Breastfeed
10am	Bottle feed
1pm	Breastfeed
4pm	Breastfeed
7pm	Bottle feed

As baby gets older, you may wish to drop more breastfeeds and introduce more bottles. If choosing to do this, ensure that you only drop one breastfeed every five days or so, no more than that. Your supply needs time to adjust and you don't want to be dealing with mastitis when also looking after your newborn baby. If you feel uncomfortable at any stage, then hand expressing or pumping a little bit of milk will take the edge off. The slower you reduce your feeds, the easier your body will adapt.

Paced Bottle-Feeding

This is a bottle-feeding technique used to try and mimic the pace of breastfeeding, the idea being that it stops your baby guzzling up the milk in a bottle and starting to prefer bottles over breast. It involves having your baby in an upright sitting position and having the bottle of milk horizontal rather than tipped downwards. This allows the baby to work harder and not simply be overwhelmed by the amount of milk coming out of the bottle teat.

As the baby drinks, the nipple of the bottle is full but the teat itself is usually only around half full due to the position of the bottle. Touch your baby's upper lip with the nipple and then allow them to open their mouth. As they open their mouth, the nipple teat goes into their mouth and baby starts to drink.

After every 20–30ml, or after a few minutes, the bottle is removed from baby's mouth and baby is given a break to wind. This stops the baby not only guzzling up all of the milk, but also allows them the feeling of their stomach gently expanding, rather than drinking everything down all in one go. It stops the bottle being drained more quickly than the breast, which in turn should stop a baby preferring the bottle over the breast.

This bottle-feeding technique can be beneficial for babies who take on a lot of wind and have reflux. That said, not all babies like the technique and if they cry more by taking them on and off, or seem bothered by it, then it could be causing more air intake and if that is the case, I would therefore recommend using a normal bottle-feeding hold for your baby.

Summary

✧ Feeding your baby does not have to be breast *or* bottle-feeding. In fact, a combination of the two can often help increase the total length of a mother's breastfeeding journey.

✧ Introducing a bottle early on is the best way to increase your baby's chance of taking one. The earlier a baby gets used to it, the less likely they will fight it later on.

✧ If baby is not accepting the bottle, have them checked for any body tension or tongue tie, which can increase their chances of not wanting to accept the bottle.

✧ Combining both breast and bottle feeds across the day allows additional flexibility for those with busy lifestyles, work commitments or with additional children around and means couples can share feeding duties.

✧ If you want to reduce the chance of baby preferring to bottle-feed, paced feeding is a feeding tool that can help reduce their chances of preferring the bottle.

A Note on Postnatal Mental Health

Hannah Mason, Sleep and Mental Health Coach

As new parents, particularly in the fourth trimester, we spend so much time and energy focusing on our baby – all the key areas this book has helpfully guided you on like feeding, sleeping and keeping your little one comfortable. But somewhere in the process, we can forget to check in on ourselves and our own needs, which is, arguably, absolutely essential in taking care of your little one too. We go through such a seismic shift physically, emotionally and mentally when we have a baby, whether it's your first or your third. Our hormones can cause a number of feelings and I just want to flag the importance of checking in with your mental health during this time, or that of your partner.

Current UK data shows that around 1 in 5 women will experience a mental health illness in the perinatal period (from conception until baby's first birthday). That might be depression, low mood, anxiety, OCD, PTSD or postpartum psychosis. Postnatal depression and postnatal anxiety are the most common for mothers and range from moderate to severe. According to the iHV (Institute of Health Visiting), depression rates for new fathers are double the national average for men in the same age group.

We are often made aware of the 'baby blues' – these tend to kick in during the first week after your baby is born, and can last until around day 14. They can be tough to navigate as you get to grips with your new baby and your own big emotions, but the teary feelings or low mood pass within a couple of weeks. If, however, you experience low mood, anxiety, feel teary or irritable for any length of time (lasting more than the initial few weeks) I implore you to speak with a close family member, friend, your health visitor or GP. People might just say 'it's just the tiredness, you'll be OK' or 'it's just the baby blues, you'll be fine!' but if you continue to feel low or anxious about parenting, your baby or any aspect of their development including their health, sleep or feeding, then you might just need some support to help you find your feet again.

Emotional upheaval following the birth of a baby is common, but this doesn't have to be your normal. If you feel that any aspect of your day-to-day life is being affected by your mood or feelings, please reach out for support. You aren't alone. You aren't failing. There is support out there for mums and dads who feel this way.

A good GP can talk you through your feelings, assess what next steps might be needed and start you on the journey to help you feeling yourself again. This might include therapy options (which aren't as scary as they sound, I promise!), or medication (there are lots that are very safe postpartum!). If you don't find support through your GP, try your health visitor or find the number of a helpful perinatal mental health charity (see page 250) that can provide a listening ear and signpost you to services.

Conclusion

As I sit here writing the very final part of this book, I can't help but feel extremely lucky to have been a part of your postnatal experience. Having a new baby is one of, if not the, most special time to be involved in someone's life and I feel honoured that you have chosen my knowledge and experience to help you navigate it.

While writing this book, I have also been on my very own postnatal journey with my third baby and this time around, I have experienced everything that is included in this book and much more. While my third experience with my daughter has been rocky, filled with feeding challenges, sensitive tummy issues and broken sleep, I can't help but feel as though it was the universe's way of gifting me even more experience and knowledge to pass on to you. Once you come out the other side of the fourth trimester, it can be easy to forget how it feels to be in it – that rawness, vulnerability and loss of identity that comes with welcoming a baby into the world, and then having them rely on you 24/7 can be very intense. It is an overwhelming time but one that passes so incredibly quickly that before you know it, you will be looking back at photos in disbelief that you did it. You fed your baby, kept them healthy and worked them out. You did it your way and no matter what stage you are in right now, you should be incredibly proud of yourself.

I have been in the parenting arena now for over 15 years, and in this time parenting itself has changed significantly. More mothers are going back to work, we have even less disposable income, and significantly less postnatal support than there used to be. With a lack of family support close by for most new parents, alongside very little professional support included in our government's post-natal support package (unless paying privately), this is a time where we really need to lean on each other for support and this is exactly where I see my role. I have spent thousands of hours in homes with new parents and the one common ground that we all share with each other is that this period of time is hard. Having a baby is hard. Becoming a parent is hard. The fourth trimester is just really hard. Yet there are so many things we can do in that time to make it easier for ourselves and that is exactly where this book comes in.

I don't want you to just have to survive on broken sleep, low mood and a baby who isn't their best self for the first few months. I want you to look back and think that it was hard, but that you enjoyed it. You got to cuddle your baby, but you also got to put them down for a nap so that you could shower. You gave them everything you needed to, but you also didn't totally lose yourself in the process. I believe you can have both a baby and a life outside of that. It doesn't have to be about having a baby strapped to you all day long who feeds every hour. There is a balance to be had, but this balance is achieved by ensuring that your baby is comfortable and contented first. There is no such thing as a bad sleeper or a baby who doesn't like to nap, and it is certainly not down to luck. There are so many variables that impact a baby's overall comfort and sleep and most of these are easily dismissed or misunderstood by the majority of the population. When you really understand babies in the way that I do, you can make your journey less stressful, full of even more joyful moments together.

This book has been designed so that you can work through it at your own pace but is easy to dip in and out of depending on which areas you are struggling with. That said, each and every chapter leads into the next and it is the whole approach combined that will give you the very best postnatal experience. If you are hoping for good sleep and a nice routine to implement, then you need a baby who is settled with their feeding and gut health thriving. If you are hoping to breastfeed your baby exclusively, then you need to ensure that they have no oral ties or tension that will impact that process. Every chapter of this book is important to every baby out there, so please give each one your time and energy. The chapter you think least applies to your baby could be the one in the end that contains the magic ingredient to make everything click into place. Be open-minded and curious and let me guide you through this journey into parenthood slowly and at a pace that you want to go at. There is no right or wrong. Choose the parts that sit right for you and use your gut instinct to help inform your decisions along the way. It may feel like you don't understand your baby just yet, but I assure you that you will and you do, it just takes time and practice. By understanding what is going on for them, you will naturally come to understand exactly what it is they need right now.

They say there is no manual when it comes to having a baby, and each and every baby is totally different from one another. There is no one-size-fits-all approach to your baby's feeding and sleep. Even on my journey as a 'baby expert', I have had to find my own way, navigating various differing professional opinions in order to work out what works best for me and the babies I have cared for, and my own little ones. I hope that in this book I have given you options in every area of your baby's wellbeing, whether that is their feeding, managing their possible reflux, the way in which you approach their sleep and everything in between. I sincerely hope that this book fills you with confidence and knowledge. Knowledge is power and by knowing the possible reasons for an unsettled or non-sleeping baby, you can start to unlock the next step for you and your baby.

Both starting and finishing this book during my third baby's fourth trimester, I want to end by giving you a little bit of heartfelt advice. Among the chaos of short naps, baby vomit and second-guessing your diet, there lies a little person whose whole world revolves around you and you only. They look to you for every little emotional interaction, for food, and to keep them safe. You are, in their eyes, still a part of them. Even on your darkest parenting days, when you have had no sleep and still have to function and get through the day, remember this. They are your biggest fan and you are doing a seriously brilliant job.

Notice the creases, the leg rolls, the tiny toes and the eyelashes. They don't stay little for long and the challenges and hurdles you are facing now that feel so big will feel so small when you look back. We can get you and your baby to a more comfortable place, but do put yourself first, because you matter too.

From one mother to another, I send you love and joy for your fourth trimester and beyond. Lean into this time. Soon you will feel like you again, and in the meantime cuddle your babies tightly. They are amazing, and so are you.

Heidi

Frequently
Asked Questions

Help! I can't put my baby down!

In this book we have explored many of the reasons as to why a baby might not want to be placed on their back in a safe sleep space. While we fully appreciate that babies like to be held and cuddled in the fourth trimester, my experience tells me that this is not usually to the extent that you can never put them down. There are so many possible reasons as to why your baby might be struggling with this and so I would encourage you to read the chapters of this book about wind, reflux, colic, oral ties and the infant gut. Understanding your baby is a journey; it will take time but there is a way of being able to put your baby down for you to be able to get a rest if that is what you would like. You matter too.

Should I use a dummy?

Some parents are very anti-dummies and others are all for them! The dummy can be a useful tool for those babies who appear to be very sucky. It helps pacify them, and in some instances calm them down too. Be mindful though that the dummy can act as an aid to help control underlying discomfort in a baby, such as reflux. When a baby sucks, it helps reduce the regurgitation that they otherwise might be experiencing. If your baby is very dummy reliant, then I suggest looking at both hunger and reflux as two possible underlying reasons as to why your baby needs a dummy.

Can I sleep my reflux baby on their tummy?

The Lullaby Trust Safe Sleeping Guidelines recommend that all babies sleep on their backs. Since the introduction of the Back to Back Sleep campaign, SIDS rates have reduced. For that reason, as a sleep coach I am not able to recommend any other sleeping position. There are potential reasons as to why you might sleep a baby on their side or front, for example with reflux, as these positions often help alleviate symptoms and baby sleeps more comfortably. This is to be decided at your own discretion and each individual family should consider the benefit and risks before making their own informed choice.

What should my baby sleep in?

As per The Lullaby Trust Safe Sleeping Guidelines, your baby's bedroom should be between 16–21 degrees. The average room temperature tends to be usually between around 19–20 degrees. The temperature in the room will influence what your baby wears.

As a general rule, between 16–18 degrees baby will likely need a vest, babygro and swaddle. If using a sleeping bag, depending on the tog you can adjust the layers accordingly. Between 19–20 degrees, a one tog sleeping bag and babygro or long-sleeved vest is recommended. In a room of 21+ degrees you may want to use a 0.5 tog sleeping bag and, in warm weather conditions, you may sleep baby in just a vest, a nappy, or a thin sleeping bag with nothing on underneath. The best way to test your baby's temperature is to feel the back of their neck and add or reduce a layer accordingly. Use your instinct as a parent when it comes to dressing your baby as this is often the best way of working it out, rather than a set standardised guideline.

What is normal versus abnormal baby poo?

Generally speaking, normal baby poo is yellow in colour, has the texture of tomato purée paste and can have seeds in it too. The consistency of poo will vary from baby to baby, with some having runnier nappies and others having more formed poo. Poo can change depending on what is going on with baby, for example if your baby is teething or unwell, mucus can appear in their poo. If they are receiving too much foremilk during breastfeeding, or have a dairy intolerance, poo can appear green. Lots of mucus or blood in poo is often a sign that your baby has either an allergy, intolerance or inflammation of the gut. Your baby should poo regularly too. If your baby is irregular, or goes a long time between pooing, then consider looking into the infant gut chapter to see if there is anything that can be done for your baby.

How do I stop my baby crying in the evening?

Crying in the evening is also known at the witching hour and can be really draining on your mental health as a parent. This sort of crying is often referred to as colic. However, we know that colic has a reason and to find those reasons takes some time. First of all, consider whether baby could be overtired from short naps across the day. If baby is getting good amounts of day time sleep and the crying persists, I recommend you look at both air intake, reflux and tummy issues as a potential reason for the witching hour. They often stop doing this as they get older, but really you don't need to just survive this crying for weeks on end. There is so much you can do about it, so have a look at the middle chapters of this book to troubleshoot.

What would happen if I did nothing when it comes to my baby's sleep?

Babies have been surviving and existing for years without sleep books. There is nothing wrong with taking the approach of just waiting it all out, going with the flow and seeing what happens as your baby grows. The only instance where I would urge you not to do this would be if baby seemed particularly uncomfortable. I think we know enough now to be able to 'unnormalise' babies crying and ensure that all babies get a chance to have a happy first few months of entry into the world. Otherwise, choose to approach parenting in the best way that suits you, whether that means co-sleeping, having a routine, not worrying about awake windows and so on... You do you, Mumma!

Can I overfeed my baby?

It has often been suggested that you cannot overfeed a breastfed baby, but from experience with reflux babies and knowing a huge amount about a baby's gut, I think it is fair to say that yes, sometimes, a baby can be overfed. When babies snack feed and cluster feed around the clock, this can overload their tummy with too much food. The gut then cannot cope and responds with symptoms that you might otherwise see as reflux or colic. Spacing feeds out can be a powerful tool in making a baby more comfortable. When it comes to formula feeding, the suggested guidelines on the back of the tins or boxes are exactly that – guidelines. Most babies will take an ounce more or less than the guidelines suggest. If your baby is taking in significantly higher amounts, their weight gain is excessive and you are concerned, speak to your doctor as this can be a sign of a baby who is drinking to counteract discomfort, often related to a milk intolerance.

How much should I play with my baby?

Your baby has very short periods of being able to be awake between feeds, so in the beginning there will not be much time for play. In this time, simply being face to face with your baby and talking to them is about as much as you need to do in terms of play. As they progress through their first few months, you will find that they will have slightly shorter feeds and longer time awake. Tummy time is an important part of their development in those early months, as is learning from you by talking and reading to them. There does not need to be any structured kind of play, and baby massage and mini yoga movements can also be a nice way of stretching them out and reducing any tension when they are very small.

Can my reflux baby learn to self-settle?

If your baby has reflux, then you will need them to be comfortable and the reflux managed to be able to work on putting them down to sleep. Your baby is unlikely to be able to fall asleep on their own, if they are regurgitating or potentially have tummy discomfort too. When a baby is laid flat on their back, this increases the chance of reflux happening for them. It is for this reason that the sleep-shaping approaches in Chapter 15 appear not to work. These approaches are solid and successful, aside from in an instance where a baby is suffering from any underlying tummy, reflux or airway issues. Once you have resolved the reflux, or medicated baby, this is a good time to start working towards self-settling.

My GP keeps dismissing my baby's symptoms, what else can I do?

This is really common and reflux having a root cause is new to many doctors, as they have to follow NICE guidelines, which look at medicating the reflux, often before looking into allergies as being a cause. If you are not getting anywhere, ask to see another doctor for a second opinion. Remember though, that you don't have to medicalise reflux unless baby is not gaining weight and in a lot of discomfort. If their symptoms are mild, you can work through this book and come to work out what is happening for them by using other health professionals such as osteopaths, lactation consultants and also your own diet and choice of formula milks too.

How do I go about starting solids with a reflux baby?

If baby's gut is healing and they are in a good place, then starting solids may go really well. However, some babies can react to certain foods when starting solids, especially high starch foods such as potatoes and more complex carbs. Start weaning slowly, introducing one food at a time and keeping a food diary for any symptoms that flare up. Use probiotics to help support your baby's gut. There is no rush and if there are foods that they are not doing well on, keep them out and come back to them at a later date. If reflux flares up then think about reducing the portion sizes your baby is having and go back to basics. You can find out lots more about weaning at positivelyparenthood.com.

Acknowledgements

To my beautiful boys and full-of-smiles baby girl, without you I would not be writing this book! My knowledge gained from your sensitive tummies and endless reflux challenges has already helped hundreds of others, and will now go on via this book to help thousands of other babies. You are my everything, and I can't wait for you to grow up and understand how your journeys helped shaped others.

To my husband, for putting up with never seeing me because I have to disappear off to my laptop every night in order to start that new project, or work on that new idea to continue my life's work of making parents' lives easier. I love you and thank you.

To my Dad – for teaching me that there are those that wonder what happened, those who watch it happen, and then there are those who make it happen. Thanks for encouraging me to be one of them. And to my Mum – for passing on your patience and love of small children. Not only that, but for rescuing me and looking after my baby girl whilst I spent time writing this for all of the other parents out there. And to my siblings, for your support as ever. Love you all.

To Ashley and Liz, my agents – the right opportunity just at the right time – thank you for all of your support. To lovely Claire for checking my wording before we even got to the first draft, whilst I wrote half sleep deprived with a newborn in arms, at the same time as trying to work out why my own newborn wouldn't feed and sleep properly (the irony!). And to Hannah for your gorgeous illustrations that make my heart happy just looking at them.

Thank you to my experts for not only contributing to this book, but for also significantly shaping the journey with my third baby too; it takes a village and new parents need to hear that there is help out there, even if it feels a little hard to come by at times.

To my amazing work colleagues, Vicki, Becky, and Josie – for continuing to help and spread the word that sleep and happy babies are possible! Your passion and support have been invaluable as I wavered through this fourth trimester whilst taking on a massive project.

To Lucy (my no 1 fan girl) and Emaneule, my career cheering champions. It means a lot that positive people like you exist in my life!

And finally, to the hundreds of babies I have slept alongside plus the thousands of babies I have helped virtually in the last decade and more, and to all of their parents too. Thank you for trusting me with your most precious cargo. You are amazing and this book exists purely out of my experience working with you all.

Thank you.

Useful Resources

Breastfeeding Support
Organisations to contact that will be able to offer virtual support if you are struggling with breastfeeding or have questions for them. You can also seek additional support via local breastfeeding café, your health visitor and local lactation consultants.

The Breastfeeding Network: www.breastfeedingnetwork.org.uk

NHS Breastfeeding Support: www.nhs.uk/conditions/baby/ breastfeeding-and-bottle-feeding/breastfeeding/

Geraldine Miskin, Breastfeeding Expert (London based): www.breastfeedingmadeeasy.co.uk

National Breastfeeding Helpline: www.nationalbreastfeedinghelpline.org.uk

Association of Breastfeeding Mothers: abm.me.uk/

La Leche League: www.laleche.org.uk

Formula Feeding
Useful websites with information on formula feeding guidelines and types of formula milks.

NHS Formula Feeding Guidelines: www.nhs.uk/conditions/baby/ breastfeeding-and-bottle-feeding/bottle-feeding/formula-milk-questions/

UNICEF Formula Feeding Guidelines: www.unicef.org.uk/babyfriendly/ wp-content/uploads/sites/2/2016/12/Parents-guide-to-infant-formula.pdf

Sleep

Online sources providing more in depth support surrounding safe sleeping guidelines and national sleep statistics as well as tailored one-to-one support.

Safe Sleeping Guidelines – The Lullaby Trust – www.lullabytrust.org.uk

Online Sleep Courses and Consultations: positivelyparenthood.com/topics/sleep/

NHS Safe Sleep Guidelines: www.nhs.uk/conditions/baby/caring-for-a-newborn/reduce-the-risk-of-sudden-infant-death-syndrome/

The Sleep Foundation – www.sleepfoundation.org

Mental Health

Postnatal Depression Support – pandasfoundation.org.uk

Dad Matters – dadmatters.org.uk

Parenting Mental Health – parentingmentalhealth.org

Mental Health and Parenting – www.nspcc.org.uk/keeping-children-safe/support-for-parents/mental-health-parenting/

Tommy's charity – www.tommys.org

MIND mental health charity – www.mind.org.uk/information-support/types-of-mental-health-problems/postnatal-depression-and-perinatal-mental-health/

Tongue Tie

Online contact details for practitioners who can help diagnose and divide tongue and lip ties.

Association of Tongue Tie Practitioners – tongue-tie.org.uk

Laser Tongue Tie Clinic – happykidsdental.co.uk

The Tongue Tie Centre – www.thetonguetiecentre.org

Lucy Rayner – Paediatric Osteopath (London) – lucytheosteopath.co.uk

Alexandra Freeman – Osteopath (London) – alexandrafreemanosteopathy.com/

Osteopathic Centre for Children (charity) – www.occ.uk.com/

Nutrition and Gut

NatureDoc Clinic (Lucinda Miller, Naturopath) – naturedoc.com/

Free to Feed, Elimination Diet Support – www.freetofeed.com/

Glossary

ACTIVE FEEDING: The process of ensuring that baby stays awake during feeding, actively taking as much milk, without falling asleep.

AWAKE WINDOW: The unique time that a baby can stay awake for before they then get tired again.

BODY TENSION: The contraction of various muscles in the body for a prolonged period of time, usually as a result of some sort of stress, such as the birth process.

COLIC: The term used when a baby is unhappy and cries a lot, with the NHS diagnosis being a baby who cries for three hours, for more than three days in a row.

COMBINATION FEEDING: Using multiple feeding methods to give baby milk – usually both breastfeeding and bottle feeding.

CONTACT NAP: A day time sleep in which baby is directly on the parent, for example upright on their chest or in arms.

CO-SLEEPING: The practice of sharing a bed with baby so that both the parent and baby are in close proximity to each other.

FOURTH TRIMESTER: The first 3–4 months of your baby's life, during which both baby and mother are getting to know each other, recovering from birth and establishing their relationship.

LIP TIE: When baby's upper lip is held down against the gum by a thick or tight frenulum, reducing baby's ability to latch and feed.

MICROBIOME: The collection of organisms that live in the digestive tract, including bacteria, fungi and viruses.

POSTNATAL DEPRESSION (PND): A mood disorder that occurs for some parents after childbirth (and can be either immediately after birth or weeks/months later).

REFLUX: The regurgitation of stomach contents into the oesophagus, which then travels back down and is swallowed by baby, or comes out as positing or sickness.

SELF-SETTLING: A baby's ability to fall asleep without needing any support from external sources (such as being rocked to sleep).

SLEEP-SHAPING: The process of implementing gentle yet effective sleep techniques to help establish positive sleep habits in the first few months of baby's life.

SNACK FEEDING: Baby taking in small amounts of milk rather than a full feed (often due to falling asleep while feeding).

TONGUE TIE: A condition in which the band of tissue holding the tongue to the floor of the mouth is too tight, thick or restricted, meaning the tongue cannot move freely and work in the most efficient way.

WINDING: The process of changing baby's position and using hand techniques to help baby bring up any burps that they may be holding on to in their stomach or digestive tract.

References

Contact Napping/Baby Wearing

Anisfeld, E., Casper, V., Nozyce, M. and Cunningham N. (1990). 'Does infant carrying promote attachment? An experimental study of the effects of increased physical contact on the development of attachment', *Child Development, 61,* 1617–1627. https://www.jstor.org/stable/1130769.

Hunziker, U.A., and Barr, R.G. (1986). 'Increased Carrying Reduces Infant Crying; A Randomized Controlled Trial', *Pediatrics 77,* 641-648. http://www.portareipiccoli.it/trial_hunziker.htm

Larimer, K. (1999) 'The Benefits of Kangaroo Care'.

Pelaez-Nogueras, M. et al (1996). 'Depressed mothers' touching increases infants' positive affect and attention in still-face interactions'. *Child Development, 67,* 1780–92. https://pubmed.ncbi.nlm.nih.gov/8890507.

Piscane, A et. al (2012). 'The use of baby carriers to increase breast-feeding duration among term infants: the effects of an educational intervention in Italy', *Acta Paediatrica 101,* 434–438.

Aerophagia

Fishbein, M., and Daniak, D. (2020). 'Aerophagia During Infant

Feeding Causing Gastroesophageal Reflux Disease like Symptoms'. *Journal of Paediatric Gastroenterology and Nutrition, 71* (2), 77–78. https://pubmed.ncbi.nlm.nih.gov/32732791.

Siegel, S.A. (2016). 'Aerophagia Induced Reflux in Breastfeeding Infants with Ankyloglossia and Shortened Maxillary Labial Frenula (Tongue and Lip Tie)'. *International Journal of Clinical Pediatrics (5)*, 6–8. https://www.theijcp.org/index.php/ijcp/article/view/246.

Body Tension

Lactation Solutions of Princeton. 'Bodywork: Gentle exercises, tummy time and massage for babies'. https:// www.lactationsolutionsof princeton.com/blog-2/2019/gentle-exercise-and-massage-for-babies.

Schwerla, F. et al (2021). 'Osteopathic treatment of infants in their first year of life: A prospective multicenter observational study (OSTINF study)'. *Complementary Medicine Research, 28* (5), 395–406. https://pubmed.ncbi.nlm.nih.gov/33601373.

Reflux Guidelines

NICE (2019). 'Gastro-oesophageal reflux disease in children and young people: diagnosis and management'. https://www.nice.org.uk /guidance/ng1.

Gut and Immunity/Health

Chau, K., et al (2014). 'Probiotics for infantile colic: a randomized double-blind placebo controlled trial investigating Lactobacillus reuteri DSM 179338'. *Journal of Paediatrics; 166,* 74–78.

Indrio, F., et al (2014). 'Prophylactic use of a probiotic in the prevention of colic, regurgitation, and functional constipation: A randomized clinical trial'. *JAMA Pediatrics, 168,* 228–233. https://pubmed.ncbi.nlm.nih.gov/24424513.

Jarbrink-Sehgal, E., and Anreasson, A. (2020). 'The gut microbiota and mental health in adults'. *Current Opinion in Neurobiology, 62,* 102–114. https://pubmed.ncbi.nlm.nih.gov/32163822.

La Flamme, A.C. and Milling, S. (2020). 'Immunological partners: the gut microbiome in homeostasis and disease'. *Immunology, 161,* 1–3. www.ncbi.nlm.nih.gov/pmc/articles/PMC7450166.

Monda, V. et al (2017). 'Exercise Modifies the Gut Microbiota with Positive Health Effects'. *Oxidative Medicine and Cellular Longevity.* https://www.ncbi.nlm.nih.gov/pmc/articles/PMC5357536.

Wu, H-J. and Wu, E. (2012). 'The role of gut microbiota in immune homeostasis and autoimmunity'. *Gut Microbes 3* (1), 4–14. https://www.ncbi.nlm.nih.gov/pmc/articles/PMC3337124.

Stages of Sleep in Utero

Suwanrath, C., and Suntharasaj, T. (2010). 'Sleep–wake cycles in normal fetuses'. *Archives of Gynaecology and Obstetrics, 281* (3), 449–54. https://pubmed.ncbi.nlm.nih.gov/19434415.

Bedtime Routines

Mindell, A. et al (2015). 'Bedtime Routines for Young Children: A Dose-Dependent Association with Sleep Outcomes'. *Sleep, 38* (5), 717–722. https://pubmed.ncbi.nlm.nih.gov/25325483.

Mindell, A. and Williamson, A. (2018). 'Benefits of a bedtime routine in young children: Sleep, development, and beyond'. *Sleep Medicine Reviews, 40,* 93–108. https://pubmed.ncbi.nlm.nih.gov/29195725.

Adenosine and Sleep

Huang, Z., Zhang, Z., and Qu, W. (2014). 'Roles of adenosine and its receptors in sleep–wake regulation'. *International Review of Neurobiology, 119,* 349–71. https://pubmed.ncbi.nlm.nih. gov/25175972.

Huang, Z., Urade, Y. and Hayaishi, O. (2011). 'The role of adenosine in the regulation of sleep'. *Current Topics in Medical Chemistry, 11 (8),* 1047–51. https://pubmed.ncbi.nlm.nih.gov/21401496.

Lazarus, M., et al (2019). 'Gating and the Need for Sleep: Dissociable Effects of Adenosine A1 and A2A Receptors'. *Frontiers in*

Neuroscience, 13. https://www.ncbi.nlm.nih.gov/pmc/articles/
PMC6650574.

Back vs Front Sleeping
Harper, R. M., Kinney, H. C., Fleming, P. J., and Thach, B. T.
(2000). 'Sleep influences on homeostatic functions: Implications for
sudden infant death syndrome'. *Respiration Physiology, 119 (2–3),*
123–132. https://pubmed.ncbi.nlm.nih.gov/10722855.

Kahn, A. et al (2003). 'Sudden infant deaths: Stress, arousal, and
SIDS'. *Early Human Development, 75* (Suppl), 147–166.
https://pubmed.ncbi.nlm.nih.gov/14693401.

4 Month Regression
Jenni, O. G., Borbely, A. A. and Achermann, P. (2003). 'Development of the nocturnal sleep electroencephalogram in human
infants'. *American Journal of Physiology, 286 (3),* 528–38.
https://pubmed.ncbi.nlm.nih.gov/14630625.

Sankupellay, M. et al (2011). 'Characteristics of sleep EEG power
spectra in healthy infants in the first two years of life'. *Clinical
Neurophysiology, 122 (2),* 236–43. https://pubmed.ncbi.nlm.nih.
gov/20650681.

Reduction in SIDS Rates
ONS, 'Unexplained deaths in infancy, England and Wales'.
https://www.ons.gov.uk/peoplepopulationandcommunity/
birthsdeathsandmarriages/deaths/bulletins/unexplaineddeathsin
infancyenglandandwales/2020.

PND in Fathers
Psouni, E., Agebjorn, J., and Linder, H. (2017). 'Symptoms of
depression in Swedish fathers in the postnatal period and development of a screening tool'. *Scandinavian Journal of Psychology, 58,* 28.
https://pubmed.ncbi.nlm.nih.gov/29052228.